Uprising in the Warsaw Ghetto

JP. Oliver

The Warsaw Ghetto Memorial by Nathan Rapaport

BER MARK

Uprising in the Warsaw Ghetto

Translated from Yiddish by Gershon Freidlin

Schocken Books · New York

First SCHOCKEN edition 1975
Copyright © 1975 by Esther Mark
Manufactured in the United States of America
Second Printing, 1976

Library of Congress Cataloging in Publication Data

Mark, Ber.
    Uprising in the Warsaw ghetto.

    Translation from Yiddish ed. of the work first published
in Polish under title: Powstanie w getcie warszawskim.
    Bibliography
    Includes index.
    1. Warsaw—History—Uprising of 1943. I. Title.
D765.2.W3M293   943.8'4   74–26913

Contents

PART I: *The History of the Uprising*

PART II: *Documents of the Uprising*

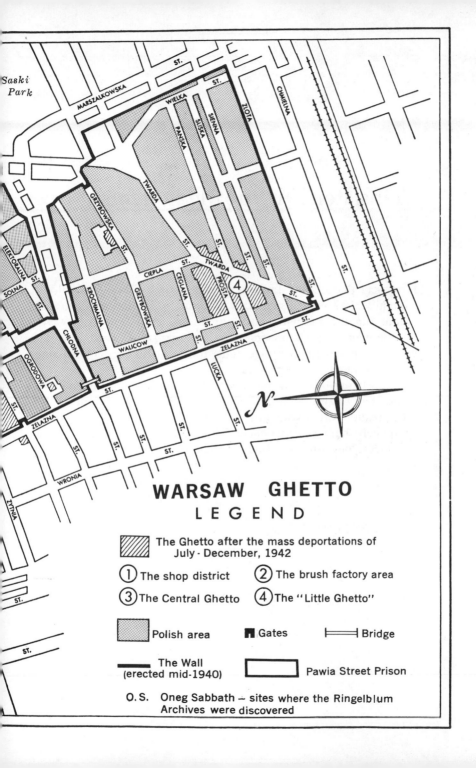

Saski Park

WARSAW GHETTO
LEGEND

The Ghetto after the mass deportations of
July - December, 1942

① The shop district   ② The brush factory area

③ The Central Ghetto   ④ The "Little Ghetto"

Polish area   ▉ Gates   ⊨⊨ Bridge

The Wall
(erected mid-1940)   ▢ Pawia Street Prison

O.S.   Oneg Sabbath – sites where the Ringelblum
Archives were discovered

Translator's Acknowledgments

I publicly thank some friends, members of the Ber Mark Book Committee, who aided significantly in the realization of this translation: Simon Federman, consulting editor, for thoroughly reviewing the manuscript; Professor Itche Goldberg, for his consistently valuable advice and encouragement; and Jacob Spiegel, coordinator and prime mover of the project.

Translating this work has been like entering a "transcendent" world—one I hardly find credible—for the past fifteen months. My own "reality" often seems trivial before it. Although I can never adequately share the experience of its heroes—living or dead—I hope that I have, nevertheless, somewhat acknowledged their glory.

With gratitude and respect,
Gershon Freidlin

New York City
Succoth, 5735

Preface

The most heroic act of armed Jewish resistance to Hitler's program of mass murder—the Warsaw Ghetto Uprising—continues to attract the attention not only of Jews but of all peoples of the world. Rarely in the history of mankind has there been such an extraordinary struggle—extraordinary in its circumstances, its superhuman heroism, and its tragic end. The example of the Warsaw Ghetto fighters remains a guiding light for all freedom-loving people; remarkably, as April 19, 1943, draws further away in time, the more inspiring become the images of the Jewish rebels, the more deeply felt is the reverence of the survivors, and the more urgent is the need to learn who these heroic men and women were and what their struggle was like.

From this steadily growing recognition of the importance of the Warsaw Ghetto Uprising stems the need to study its history in more depth and without interference. And since, in the time that has passed, ever-richer sources of documents, memoirs, and other materials have become available, historians of the Uprising are faced with the challenge of revising, complementing, and extending their previous scholarship—improving their works and gradually developing a more complete perspective on that fateful event.

Such is the case with the previous edition of this work, which was published in Polish in 1959.[1] Since then, many new documents have been discovered in Yiddish, Polish, and German. Eyewitnesses and

[1] Ber Mark, *Walka in zaglada warszawkiego getta.* Warsaw, 1959.

surviving participants of the Uprising who had previously kept silent have revealed their recollections of those horrible and heroic days. Thanks to these historical finds and personal revelations the present edition was made possible.

Here, the author tries to avoid the shortcomings of the 1959 edition. The events that led to the Uprising are dealt with only as they are necessary to understand the Jews' dream of armed resistance in the Warsaw Ghetto. The emphasis is on the intensity, duration, and spirit of the battles fought on the ruined landscape of the burning Ghetto. For the revolt did not end in capitulation or decisive defeat; it ebbed as the physical strength and weaponry of the Jewish fighters was exhausted and died out only as the rebels succumbed to the overwhelming strength of the enemy. But sporadic confrontations with the German police and SS continued for a much longer time than originally reported by either Jewish sources or in the communiqués of the police and SS commandant of the Warsaw district, Juergen Stroop. Other German documents contend that skirmishes amidst the ruins of the Ghetto occurred even in July of 1943, and a Polish source cites evidence of armed groups of Jews in the razed Ghetto area in 1944!

Equipped then, with the most up-to-date information—a listing of which is included at the end of this volume—we examined anew the saga of that heroic and tragic struggle. In the chapters that follow, the reader will come to understand that the Uprising was not a spontaneous outbreak of resistance, but rather the product of a long period of psychological and practical preparation. And not only the Uprising itself—the culmination of a long-time dream of resistance—but the historic vision it so nobly represented, burgeoned not on barren ground, but in a culture made fertile by the determination and will of many generations of Jews to resist any onslaught upon their biological, national, and economic integrity. Within the Jewish community of Poland, and eastern Europe generally, two lines perpetually crossed paths: in one instance, the impulse to self-defense, resistance, and struggle continually encountered the tack of accommodation and desertion; in like fashion, admonitions to join ranks for the emancipation of mankind met head-on with overwhelming fear of the Nazi overlord and the devastating effects of spiritual isolation in the ghettos. In the most elementary terms, the rebels found themselves squarely opposed to the most entrenched "power" of the Ghetto: the *Judenrat.*

However, the social forces that spawned the Jewish Fighting Organization had steeped the rebel Jews in the tactics of proletarian self-defense used against the pogroms of czarism; in the spirit of the great political battles against fascism and anti-Semitism of the period between the two wars; in the legacies of Hersz Lekert, Pinchas Daszewski, Baruch Szulman, Szolem Szwarczbard, and Noftoli Botwin; and in the tradition of the Maccabees and all national, progressive, and revolutionary movements in Jewish history and in the history of mankind.

The pioneers of active Jewish resistance in the Warsaw Ghetto—and in the other Jewish ghettos as well—regarded their effort as part of the general battle against Hitler and fascism: to secure a decent future for the world. The underground press of the Ghetto printed extensive reports of the resistance against the Nazi occupation forces throughout Poland and all across the face of bleeding Europe. But before all else, the leaders of Jewish resistance frankly and courageously told their fellow Ghetto inmates of the suffering and imminent destruction of the Jewish people under the Nazi axe, at the same time stressing that the logical response should not be despair and submission, but readiness to sound the alarm, take up arms, and, if need be, sacrifice oneself to resist the enemy. All their traditions pointed in but one direction: in the very shadow of death the dream of resistance became reality, became the heroic Uprising that shook all Jewry and people of good will.

BER MARK

Warsaw, 1963

I

The History of the Uprising

1

Eve of the Uprising

Ghetto Conditions in Early 1943

One of the most tragic aspects of the Warsaw Ghetto Uprising is that, when the unequal battle finally took place in April 1943, the once-massive Jewish population of Poland in general, and Warsaw specifically, no longer existed. In twenty-one months, from October 1940 till July 1942, almost one hundred thousand Warsaw Ghetto Jews died—of hunger, epidemic, superhuman slave labor in concentration camps, or through mass execution. From July 22, 1942, to the middle of September 1942, alone, three hundred thousand of them were either deported to the Treblinka camp by the Germans or their collaborators, or shot on the spot.

Except for isolated sabotage, individual acts of resistance, and the Jewish underground-initiated assassination attempt on Joseph Szerinski (Szenkman), Ghetto police commandant, by Israel Kanal, there was no mass resistance during the aforementioned period of deportation. Activists' two-year dream of armed uprising was destined to be fulfilled only after the Jewish population had been reduced to a tenth its original size, and as the remnant stood facing its own grave.

At the beginning of 1943, the Ghetto was no longer a unit. The conqueror had sliced it into three sections, categorizing but two of them as economically productive. One, the "shop" district, formed a square bordering on the even side of Leszno Street, and on

Nowolipie, Nowolipki, Karmelicka, and Smocza streets. It contained work places manned by Jewish slave labor and managed by German entrepreneurs. The second was the huge brush factory blocks with its workshops on Swientojerska and Walowa streets and part of Franciszkanska Street.

The third section was called Central Ghetto. Among its streets were Wolynska, Szczeszliwa, Ostrowska, Niska, Stawki, Nalewki, Gesia, Dzika (Zamenhofa), Mila, and Muranowska. It contained some factories and the offices of the *Judenrat*.[1]

Spaces between the three main sections were out of bounds to Jews, but many lived there illegally; they were the so-called wild areas. These streets, and even some "legal" ones, resembled the shambles of a permanent pogrom. The cobblestones were covered with broken furniture and cracked windowpanes; bits of torn clothing, rags, and feathers from ruined bedding blew over them. Houses lay empty and abandoned. In January of 1943 the Germans had attempted another deportation and succeeded in leading away thousands of Jews and destroying their dwellings.

Just before the Uprising, the cut-up Ghetto together with the "Little Ghetto" on Prosta Street housed some legal Jewish residents; in the wild areas and in the shop district an equal number of "illegal" ones were to be found.[2] The latter were those without work identification papers—the "unproductives," refugees, and escapees from Treblinka or from trains bound there. These illegitimates had been marked for deportation but hid and existed like pursued beasts.

The Ghetto captives, legal as well as illegal, were an unfortunate mass. They were the remains of a broken people and detached limbs of torn families: parents without children, children without parents, husbands without wives—the women having been sent to the *Umschlagplatz* [3]—and miserable widows whose husbands had perished. These were persons thrown to cruel fate, permanent mourners who

---

[1] *Judenrat:* Name of Jewish councils set up by Nazis in occupied territories—*trans.*

[2] The population of Warsaw in March 1943 was 974,000, of which 915,000 were Poles, 17,000 Germans, and 35,000 (legal) Jews.

[3] Terminus of railway spur near the Ghetto where deportees were gathered for removal from the city—*trans.*

soberly concluded that deportation or a gas chamber death would not be their lot.

The majority of the survivors were now determined not to go meekly to the transport trains. Feverishly they prepared bunkers and weapons and finally began to give their attention and trust to the Jewish Fighting Organization's summons to battle.

The Anti-Fascist Bloc

No matter how tragic the circumstances of the Warsaw Ghetto Uprising, the act of uprising was not one of despair. Armed confrontation for the last cadres of Ghetto prisoners was the direct result of a long process, realization of a dream not only of self-defense but also of enlisting in the fighting ranks of the local and international revolutionary movement. The contents of the underground press in the Warsaw Ghetto from 1940–42—in itself a popular front within the Ghetto underground—attest to this. The majority of illegal publications, including the Anti-Fascist Bloc's own organ, *Der Ruf,* attempted to arouse the populace to rebellion.

The very name of this first communal organization—Anti-Fascist Bloc—indicates that the pioneers of active resistance in the Warsaw Ghetto had greater ideas behind their opposition than mere self defense: namely, general revolt against fascism. The Anti-Fascist Bloc had a clear program for national and social liberation. The Bloc considered the battle for which it agitated as the Jewish people's contribution to the overall anti-Nazi struggle of freedom-loving mankind. Its member bodies were the Polish Workers Party (P.P.R.), Hashomer Hatzair, Left and Right Labor Zionists, and Hechalutz.

Some of the chief activists intimately associated with the Bloc were Joseph Lewartowski, Pinya Kartin ("Andrzej Schmidt"), Shmul Meretyk, Joseph Kaplan, Shakhne Zagan, and Mordekhai Tenenboim ("Tamarov")—all killed by the Nazi murderers between May and August, 1942.

The most prominent of the military instructors who continued in their capacity even after the Bloc's demise included Kartin and Mordekhai Anielewicz. Kartin, a former captain in the International

Brigades during the Spanish Civil War, arrived in Poland in January 1942, as a parachutist from Moscow. Mordekhai Anielewicz, also an instructor in the Gymnasium where he had been studying before the war, had been a leader in encounters against perpetrators of Polish Fascist pogroms. Other Bloc instructors were Gershon Alef ("Bolek"), Hersz Lent, Victor Margolies, and Itzhak Cukierman. Also worthy of mention is the involvement of heroic women representing various organizations: Chaike Grossman, Zosia Zatorska, Niuta Teitelboim, the sisters Chana and Frume Platnycka, Faygl Peltel-Miedzyrzecka.

Irena Adamowicz, a Polish scouting leader, along with others, carried out dangerous courier missions on the "Aryan" side of the Ghetto and in the provinces. Through the authorization of the Jewish underground she visited the ghettos in Bialystok, Vilna, Kovno, and Shavel, where she delivered words of encouragement and rebellion and brought back information to the Warsaw Ghetto underground.

The Jewish Fighting Organization

Between the heyday of the Anti-Fascist Bloc and the rise of the Jewish Fighting Organization flowed a sea of blood that gushed forth from Warsaw Ghetto prisoners in the horrible liquidation of July–September 1942.

The idea of a combat organization was born in July at the height of the liquidation and brought to life in October. On December 2, a charter was adopted that set forth the body's purposes: (a) "Organizing for the defense of the Jewish population of Warsaw against the occupation force's acts of annihilation and (b) protection of the Jewish Ghetto masses against the occupying force's lackeys." (From the Introduction to the Charter)

Commander-in-chief was Anielewicz, a twenty-four-year-old Hashomer Hatzair activist. Other members were Hersz Berlinski (Left Labor Zionist), Marek Edelman (Jewish Labor Bund), Itzhak Cukierman (Hechalutz), and Michal Roisenfeld (Polish Workers Party).

The work of the group from inception to the beginning of the Uprising was multifaceted but all objectives were directed toward an unavoidable armed clash with the Nazis. The work had six focal points:

1. Spreading the idea of active resistance among the masses. The catchword heard throughout the Ghetto was "We will not relinquish one Jew."

2. Mobilizing and training determined fighters. Selection had to be strict, because spies, Gestapo agents, and informers were floating everywhere. In one instance, a Jewish agent betrayed to the Gestapo two Jewish fighters, Itzhak Konski and Szymon Leventhal, who had stepped out of the Ghetto to buy weapons. No torture could make them talk; they willingly gave up their young lives.

Extreme caution was demanded of the Fighting Organization, which actually became a school for character. Aside from the organized fighters themselves, assigned to highly clandestine cells, trial members, who first had to pass through a candidacy stage, were also accepted.

3. Collecting weapons. Much energy was spent toward this end. The first modest grant of weapons was received free from the outside, from the Polish Workers Party and a Polish guerrilla group, the People's Guard. Next came help from the Polish socialist movement. The richest underground group, the Land Army (A.K.), with headquarters in London with the Polish government-in-exile, at first made difficulties. As late as January 1943, the commander-in-chief of A.K., "Grot" (Gen. Stefan Rowecki) wrote secretly to London that the "Jewish Communist" circles in the Ghetto (meaning the Fighting Organization) wanted weapons, but he was not sure that they could make use of them, and perhaps they should not be given any. Later A.K. did provide some arms, but by that time the insurgents had taken to manufacturing their own or buying them from German and Italian marauders at outlandish prices.

4. Collecting funds. The Jews as a rule gave willingly. There were, however, new Ghetto profiteers and some of the earlier rich who tried to evade responsibility. Such despicables were arrested by the Fighting Organization and "taxed" or forced to contribute. An exemplary merchant of means who donated vast sums and fully

supported the fighters was Abraham Gefner, a noted activist for Jewish causes.

5. Extermination campaign against traitors, Gestapo agents, and informers. This included carrying out of death sentences. Indeed the strongest effect upon Ghetto victims was made by the executions of the old German spy, Dr. Alfred Nossig; Jacob Lejkin, leader of the traitorous *Ordnungsdienst* (Ghetto police); Israel First, Gestapo undercover man; and other agents. Jewish bullets also fell upon Germans—SS men and military police. There came a point where the enemy feared to go alone in Ghetto streets.

6. Finally, contact with the Polish underground and the last islands of survivors of other Polish-Jewish communities. Through representatives (Aryeh Wilner, and after March 1943, Itzhak Cukierman) on the "Aryan" side, the Organization was in constant comradely contact with the People's Guard. Relations with the Land Army were much stiffer and only through the efforts of Polish democrats like Henryk Wolinski, Henryk Kaminski, and members of the Council for Jewish Assistance (in which two Jews—Dr. Leon Feiner for the Jewish Labor Bund and Dr. Abraham Berman for the Jewish National Committee—also participated) were connections maintained. These contacts allowed secret messages and SOS alarms to pass to Jewish groups outside Poland, who then gave back large sums of money for weapons and aided in escape of Jews hiding on the Aryan side.

Shortly after its creation, the Jewish Fighting Organization was able to prove its mettle in battle, and when necessary, with primitive arms: axe, beam, and cobblestone. When, from January 18 to 22, 1943, the Germans staged an unexpected effort to deport remaining Jews, the Organization rebelled—almost with bare hands. After dragging out a number of Jews the Nazis had to leave the Ghetto in shame, carrying with them their own twenty dead and forty wounded. For the first time they glimpsed Jewish faces, not backs. In commemoration of this little victory, the Polish-Jewish poet Wladislaw Szlengel wrote his famous "Counterattack" and Itzhak Katznelson dedicated a part of "Lid vegn oisgehargeten yiddishn folk" ("Song of the Murdered Jewish People").

Hardly two months later, on March 13, a deed raised the prestige of the Fighting Organization among Ghetto inmates and the Polish underground, and brought concern to the enemy. A Jewish fighter had shot a German *Luftwaffe* officer in the street. In return, Karl-Georg Brand, Gestapo appointee over the Jews, brought in SS men who carried out a slaughter on Mila Street. The incidents took place on a Saturday; hence the day was called by Jews "The Bloody Sabbath." For a second time Jewish warriors offered active resistance.

Yiddisher Militerisher Farband and Other Groups

In addition to the Fighting Organization, other battle groups were formed, the largest of which was the Yiddisher Militerisher Farband (Jewish Military Alliance). The difference between the Fighting Organization and the Farband is that the former had an anti-fascist orientation and had leftist worker elements at its core; the latter was self-defense oriented and comprised chiefly of bourgeois youth, former combatants, and members of the Betar—the Zionist Revisionist Youth Organization. The Farband was joined later by groups of porters and smugglers headed by Yossl (Janek) Piko, "Krzywonos," and Pawel Rodi (Pinya Beshtimt).

Another important difference between the two groups lay in the Organization's representing a broader spectrum of forces within the Jewish community. This fact underlay its claim to represent that community in both internal and external affairs, a status acknowledged by all sectors of the Polish underground. Authoritative factions of the latter recognized a coordinating commission of member bodies of the Fighting Organization.

The Farband over the course of its existence underwent several transformations. In 1939 veterans of the "September campaign" [4] organized as an underground group and called themselves Swit (Dawn). They soon set up contact with a Polish underground association headed by Col. Andzhei Petrikowski,[5] who appointed a special Polish committee led by Maj. Henryk Iwanski to maintain

---

[4] "September campaign" refers to the effort to resist the Nazi invasion of Poland, September 1939—*trans.*
[5] Petrikowski is of Jewish descent, related to early Zionist leader, Nahum Sokolow.

relations with and support the Jewish body. Later Swit broadened its base and changed the name to Yiddisher Kampfs Farband.

In October, 1942, the Kampfs Farband had 150 trained members organized by sections. The Polish group of Maj. Iwanski provided it with much weaponry and ammunition—especially grenades, also machine guns. Such aid was also received through another source: a Polish democratic underground organization called Arpand. Farband membership grew to four hundred by the beginning of 1943, and succeeded in a number of attempts on the lives of SS men and Jewish Gestapo agents. Their name now became "Division of Revenge" and right before the Uprising, Yiddisher Militerisher Farband.

At the head stood two commanders: David Apelboim ("Jablonski," "Kowal," "Mietek"), a former lieutenant in the Polish army of religious background and from a family of rich fur dealers; and Pawel Frenkl, a student. Heading Farband communal activities were Dr. David Wdowinski, Dr. Michael Strykowski, and an attorney, David Szulman.

The Farband distinguished itself prior to the Uprising by two actions which won it much public sympathy. The first took place on April 16, at a literary evening held in a Jewish working-class neighborhood by Wladislaw Szlengel, famous for his poems about the Ghetto and resistance activities. Money collected there was then distributed to impoverished Jews for the approaching Passover.

Amidst the proceedings, a group of very well-armed, masked Jews broke into the room and handed over to the poet 10,000 zlotys for abandoned Ghetto children. After announcing their affiliation with the Farband they left immediately. They made a very strong impression that evening, not only by the size of their financial contribution, but also by the mere fact of existence of an armed body that could protect Jews.

The Farband's next significant accomplishment was rooting out an organization of spies and provocateurs, Zagew,[6] Zydowska Gwardia Wolno (Jewish Liberation Militia). Zagew had been installed in the Ghetto by the Gestapo a short time before the rebel-

---

[6] Zagew: Literally, Torch—*trans.*

lion. Its job was to spy on the Jewish underground, compile a list of Jewish Communists, and stir up enough confusion to bring about a premature uprising that would allow the Germans to drown the resistance in blood and to do away with Ghetto inmates. Connected with this band of provocateurs was Abraham Gancwajch, who turned up once again in the Ghetto in collusion with one sinister "Capt. Lewicki," also known as "Capt. Lencki." There he set up the so-called Polish Battle Organization with goals similar to Zagew's.

Within a few weeks the Farband liquidated all three departments of Zagew, which included Jewish traitors, Gestapo agents, and other Jews who had been seized on the Aryan side and forced to do dirty work to save their skins. In all, fifty-nine persons were executed after a trial by secret Jewish court.

In their efforts to procure arms, Farband emissaries first reached the western railway terminal of the city; from there they proceeded to the distant suburban neighborhood, Targowek, where they arranged a secret meeting place at an arsenal. Another route for importing weapons led through a sewer between the even side of Karmelicka Street, on the Aryan side, to the Farband bunker in the Ghetto at Karmelicka 5. From there weapons were transported to headquarters at Muranowska 7. Another tunnel, 50 meters long, connected headquarters with the Aryan side. Through that, emissaries left to buy weapons and Polish underground fighters would enter to deliver grenades, pistols, and bullets.

The Farband raised funds in ways similar to the Fighting Organization: through donations and expropriations, and Abraham Gefner. Food, especially zwieback, was supplied largely by baking firms belonging to Bleiman Brothers or the Lopato Family. A special Farband service dealt with bands of thieves from the Polish underworld who would come into the Ghetto for "special entertainment" —robbery, assault, and rape.

Negotiations were continually held with the Fighting Organization for either uniting the two bodies or at least coordinating their work. By the eve of the rebellion agreement of the latter type was indeed reached. In the Fighting Organization's overall plan for Ghetto defense one of the Farband battle stations, that in the housing blocks at the corner of Muranowska and Nalewki, was acknowledged. In addition to this position, the Farband had armed groups at other spots. As part of the agreement with the Fighting Organization, the Farband group at the shop area gave its partner a case of grenades. At the last moment before the actual Uprising the function of emissary to the Farband from Fighting Organization headquarters at Mila 18 was assumed by Eliyahu Rutkowski, an educator. Pawel Frenkl served as coordinator from the Farband.

Other organized groups were active in the Ghetto, for example, the porters' groups at Mila and neighboring streets. One group was led by Gotlieb, a Jewish officer of Polish People's Army (P.A.L.), which stood close to the Polish Socialist Party (P.P.S.). Gotlieb also maintained contact with the Jewish Labor Bund and smuggled arms into the Ghetto.

Armed Might of the German Goliath

The Nazi security force in Warsaw was not ignorant of what brewed in the Ghetto. In January, February, and March 1943, it had come to feel the might of Jewish fighters on its own skin. As a result, Himmler sought to make an end of the Ghetto. On February 16, 1943, he sent out a liquidation order to higher SS and police leaders of the Cracow region. The German factory owners Toebbens, Schultz, and others urged Jewish workers to move willingly with their machinery to SS camps at Trawniki and Poniatow (in the Lublin region) where "they would live out the war in peace."

When the Fighting Organization retaliated against this and shop workers took to sabotage, the Germans decided upon forced deportation. The job was to be completed by April 19, in order that Warsaw would be *Judenrein* for the 20th, Hitler's birthday. To ward off any Jewish resistance SS General Juergen Stroop was brought in to aid the Warsaw police and SS leader von Sammern. Stroop was well trained and had very recent anti-insurgency experience fighting Soviet partisans in the eastern Ukraine. Himmler himself visited Warsaw on the 16th for confidential meetings. With him was General Schnebel, a top Gestapo figure.

The Germans made ready the following military resources for the liquidation of the Ghetto:

Over two thousand soldiers and officers of *Waffen SS*.

Three *Wehrmacht* divisions, both artillery and sappers. The artillery would barrage the houses, as the sappers set off explosions throughout the Ghetto.

Two German police battalions totaling 234 officers and enlisted men.

367 Polish police, so-called *Granatowa,* enlisted men and officers.

35 security policemen.

A 337-member battalion of the so-called *Oskaren,* Ukrainian and Latvian Fascists from SS auxiliary troop detachments.

These personnel totaled 2,842. In addition at least seven thousand SS troops, police, and gendarmes were mobilized in the city in reserve, and double that amount in the surrounding area, lest flames of rebellion leap to the Aryan side.

Excellently armed, the Germans had the latest equipment at their disposal: machine guns, endless ammunition, tanks, armored trucks, cannon, and planes. Movement was free, conditions sanitary, and food plentiful. The leaders were both formally schooled and field-trained in battle.

Some of the leaders and their charges were: SS Lt. Col. Bellwid, heading armored detachments of SS grenadiers; SS Capt. Plaenk, a completely motorized cavalry company of *Waffen SS;* German police forces were commanded by Maj. Sternhagel, Maj. Otto Bundke (Berlin police captain in 1936), Maj. Scheffe, Capt. Oskar Cizenis, Capt. Ederer, Lt. Diehl, Lt. Strobel, SS 2nd Lt. Karl Schnerzer, and others like SS Maj. Jesuiter, staff supervisor, and Josef Belesche, a security police officer with similar experience in occupied Soviet Union. These men had been tested under fire both in that country and France.

The Ukrainian–Latvian Fascists were commanded by both German and Latvian officers. Of the former were Rolkman, Urlich, Huselman, Klassen; the latter: Bajerlson, Lautheller, Geibler, and Pirletzkis.

The entire operation was headed at first by the SS and police chief of the Warsaw District, SS Brig. Gen. and Police Col. Ferdinand von Sammern Frankenegg. Succeeding him was a special deputy from Heinrich Himmler, SS and Police Brig. Gen. Juergen Stroop. Stroop was assisted by SS Lt. Col. Dr. Ludwig Hahn, chief in Warsaw of both Security Police and Security Forces, a bureau subordinate to the Gestapo.

In the action against the Jews important roles were played by one of Hahn's deputies, SS 2nd Lt. Karl-Georg Brand, head of the Jewish division of the Warsaw Gestapo, and SS 2nd Lt. Franz Konrad. The latter was in charge of *Werterfassung,* a thievish SS agency responsible for the collection of Jewish valuables, and was assigned to Maj. Gen. Odilo Globocnik, chief of *Einsatz Reinhardt.* That institution was responsible for the deportation of Jews and the SS concentration camps in the Lublin district, and continued till the end to handle the liquidation of Jewish property. Globocnik, a Lublin resident, did not stay long at the Ghetto battle site but turned the work over to his associate Georg Michelson, one of the worst specimens of Nazi bestiality.

The Nazi staff benefited from the aid and advice of Dr. Ludwig Fischer, governor of the Warsaw District; Gen. Rosus, commandant of its *Wehrmacht* garrison; Higher SS and Police Chief Gen. Friedrich-Wilhelm Krueger of Cracow; the Nazi party apparatus, plus the entire military and civilian populations of Warsaw.

In brief, united against surviving Jews in Warsaw were the combined military, police, political, and economic resources of the Nazi occupation forces and their collaborators. Among the latter, ingrained anti-Semites, were Ukrainian and Latvian Fascists, Polish police, and the *shmaltzovniks.*[7] Also, underground Fascist cadres like Narodowe Sily Zbrojne (National Armed Forces); Miecz i Plug, (Sword and Plow), Konfederacja Narodu, and the like aided the Nazi plan.

---

[7] Extortionists who drew money from Jews in exchange for promises not to report them to Nazis, then betrayed them anyway—*trans.*

Rebel Strength

Against forces armed from head to toe stood the poorly equipped, inexperienced, miniscule, and starving bands of Ghetto warriors, with organized forces comprised of six hundred members from the Jewish Fighting Organization, four hundred from the Farband, plus the porter groups.

Although the initiative of the Uprising lay in the hands of the organized, thousands more participated spontaneously—assembled through bunkers, professions, or by chance. In "wild" groups each individual purchased his own weapons, and was often better supplied than his organized counterpart.

The Fighting Organization concentrated its divisions in three areas: Central Ghetto, the brush factory zone, and the shops. The first covered Nalewki, Gesia, Zamenhofa, Mila, and neighboring streets. Commanders were Zekhariah Artszteyn, Berl Broide, Aaron ("Pawel") Briskin, Mordekhai ("Merdek") Growas, Levi Grozalc, David Hochberg, Henryk Zylberberg, Joseph Farber, and Leyb ("Lutek") Rotblat.

The second contingent deployed itself in the brush factory area: Swientojerska and Walowa streets and part of the odd-numbered side of Franciszkanska. Here fighting groups were led by Hersz Berlinski, Jurek Blones, Henokh Gutman, Jurek Grynszpan, and Jacob Praszker—under the general leadership of Marek Edelman.

The third concentration was in the shop area: Leszno, Nowolipie, Nowolipki, and Smocza streets. Here were stationed groups under Itzhak Bloiszteyn, Benjamin Wald, Joshua Winogron, Meir Mairowicz, David Nowodworski, Jacob ("Jacek") Feigenblat, Hersz Kawe, Wolf Rozowski, and Adam ("Janek Bialy") Szwarcfus. Eliezer Geller served as coordinator here for the central staff.

One begins to see how the Fighting Organization's central staff was deployed. Two of its members, Berlinski and Edelman, served the brush factory. A third, Itzhak Cukierman was the representative on the Aryan side to both sectors of the Polish underground. His task was to get maximum aid. Young Frania Beatus ran as courier between Cukierman and central headquarters. In May 1943 she was to commit suicide in despair over the situation of Ghetto warriors for whom bringing real relief was an impossible task.

Commander-in-chief Anielewicz remained at headquarters with staff member Michal Roisenfeld and other close associates like Israel Kanal and Aryeh Wilner, former emissary on the Aryan side. Kanal carried out the rebels' first successful assassination.

The Fighting Organization arsenal contained primarily grenades, bottles with explosive fluid (the so-called Molotov cocktails), bombs, pistols, rifles, and mines. Later additional weaponry was taken in battle from Germans. Ammunition was sparse. The Farband was far better endowed, especially with grenades and guns. Just its largest detachment, stationed on Muranowska Street, possessed three hundred grenades, eight automatic rifles, one light and two heavy machine guns, and several thousand bullets. Many Farband fighters wore German uniforms prepared beforehand.

Chief battle station was on Muranowska Street, with units led by Roman Weinsztok, Szyja Teneboim, Lipszyc, and Leyb Rodal —under the general command of David Apelboim and Pawel Frenkl. Farband groups of fifteen to forty persons also operated in the Central Ghetto and were headed by Chaim Federbusz at Gesia, Pawia, and Zamenhofa streets; by Yosl Piko at Mila Street; and by Leizer Staniewicz, Szyja Wolf, and Binsztok at Nalewki and Franciszkanska streets. In the brush factory area were groups under Chaim Lopato, Abraham Rodal (Leyb's brother), and Pinya Beshtimt (Pawel Rodi).

The Farband shop district group was quartered at Karmelicka 5 and led by Nuson Szulc, Pinkhas Taub ("Wilek," grandson of Hasidic grand rabbi of Modzyc), and David Szulman. There is also some data on the activities of the "wild" groups that came into being spontaneously or under the influence of organized fighting bands, especially in the later phases of the conflict. They were directed by Moishe "Bolshevik," Szymon Melon, Szymon Koifman, and many others.

Strategy of Resistance

The Uprising leadership concluded that face-to-face confrontation with the Germans would finish the Jews as soon as they started. It was thus decided to attack the enemy from buildings located at crossroads. Shooting at invading Germans marching in the open street from hidden spots behind windows, house walls, or in attics was more comfortable for the rebels. At the same time, they built underground bunkers to escape bombardment and tunnels to move about within the Ghetto, or possibly to reach the other side. The civilian population, preparing a more passive resistance, built bunkers and stored food.

Day and night the Ghetto made ready to receive the enemy with active and supportive resistance. "They figured out," wrote Ghetto historian Emmanuel Ringelblum, "that the battle was between a fly and an elephant, but national pride demanded Jews offer resistance and not allow themselves to be led wantonly to slaughter."

Anielewicz sensed what the outcome of the unequal confrontation would be; yet he and others hoped all Warsaw would respond to the shots in the Ghetto, and revolt would spread throughout the city. Indeed, the enemy dreaded the same, and therefore marched into the Ghetto with maximum force.

Anielewicz's hope never materialized.

The Ghetto lay in watchful anticipation. Dead silence reigned over the streets and homes, as before a storm.

2

Outbreak of Rebellion:
April 19, 1943

Leyl Shimurim (Night of Vigil): April 18

Sunday, April 18, a conference was held at headquarters of police and SS leadership to discuss details of the morrow's planned daybreak assault on the Ghetto. That same day at 2:00 P.M., SS and German police received the order to be on alert. A similar command was issued the Polish *(Granatowa)* police, which at 6:00 P.M. surrounded the Ghetto area with heavy patrols. Within the hour enemy preparations were already known to the Ghetto, the staffs of the Jewish Fighting Organization and the Farband.

That evening at the Fighting Organization staff bunker an instructional session was held for group leaders of the Central Ghetto, under chairmanship of Mordekhai Anielewicz. There, weapons distribution was completed. Baskets with bottles of incendiary fluid were passed out, in addition to which each group received grenades and ammunition. Food and cyanide were also given.

The slogan "Jan-Warsawa" traveled from mouth to mouth— both password and battle alert signal. Group commanders then forbade fighters to leave their positions. House gates were barricaded with furniture and street passage was blocked. Bags of sand and cushions were placed before windows to deflect bullets. The mood among fighting groups was of exemplary order, calm, and self-control. The night of April 18 was one of vigil.

According to ancient Jewish tradition it was a night of vigil in another sense: the night of the first Seder, Passover 5703. In the Ghetto were more persons than usual; many Jews had sneaked over from the Aryan side in order to celebrate the Seder in a Jewish environment.

At 2:00 A.M. the ring of guards around the Ghetto was reinforced by German police and Latvian–Ukrainian SS auxiliary formations. Every 25 meters a guard stood with a heavy machine gun. Groups of Latvian Fascists and Polish police moved by columns into the Ghetto, advanced through the streets, and headed for the *Umschlag-platz*. During the night, Gestapo bigwig Brand made a check of Ghetto streets in his black automobile the Jews knew so well. Except for reconnaissance squads, no living soul among the Jewish fighters appeared on Ghetto streets.

The rebels prepared to properly receive the enemy. They hung banners at prominent spots, red, white and blue, and white and red. In one place a group unfurled a white and blue flag with a red five-cornered star in the middle. On the walls that bordered the Aryan side, as on Swientojerska Street, a banner was raised with an appeal to the Polish population to take solidarity action on behalf of the Jewish fighters.

According to the plan of SS and Police Chief von Sammern, the Central Ghetto—"Ghetto remains" in the Nazi murderers' parlance —was to disappear with the first firing. The shop and brush factory areas were to be ignored for the time being. The expectation was that the Jews, seeing the "Ghetto remains" rebellion choked by fire and blood, would go voluntarily, without difficulty, to deportation.

The staffs of the Jewish Fighting Organization and the Farband concentrated attack forces at three points: first, the corner of Nalewki and Gesia streets, near the entrance to the chief Ghetto artery; second, the crossing at Zamenhofa and Mila streets; and third, the intersection of Muranowska and Nalewki streets, opposite Muranowski Square. In this manner the first battle line was planned as a triangle to protect the Central Ghetto streets. Defense of the first two points lay in the hands of Jewish Fighting Organization groups, and the third, with the Farband.

Monday, April 19, von Sammern led armed troops into the Central Ghetto through the Nalewki Gate, having planned the following troop deployment: one detachment was to stop in the middle of Nalewki Street to begin seizure and deportation actions; a second would continue through Gesia to Zamenhofa Street, in other words, to the second major artery, then proceed further.

The Germans feared for their lives, feared the bullets of Jewish fighters; hence, in the first rows they sent detachments of Latvian Fascists and the remainder of the *Ordungsdienst* (Ghetto Police). Such Jewish police refusing to participate in the action or who attempted escape were shot in Gestapo headquarters at Zelazna 103.

Only behind the vanguard of Latvian and Jewish police did columns of Germans and Ukrainians move forward. Their march resembled a military formation in all its details. First came motorcycles, then trucks with infantry and heavy machine guns; finally ambulances, a field kitchen, and field telephone apparatus. In addition, the German command brought twelve armored cars into the Ghetto. On the main streets tables and benches were set up, and on the tables, telephones. The entire scene gave the appearance of a full-fledged military campaign.

Von Sammern's divisions, though, did not get far—they were halted at two locations: at the corner of Nalewki and Gesia, and at the Zamenhofa–Mila intersection. As Nazi bigwigs were later to admit, "the Jewish rebellion was unanticipated, amazingly forceful, and a great surprise." The German forces were simply thrown out of the Ghetto—so commented SS Gen. Stroop, who wrote the following in his report to Krueger and Himmler: "At our first entry into the Ghetto the Jews and Polish bandits [1] succeeded through a planned armed attack in pushing back our offensive forces together with the tanks and armored cars."

We read about this initial Jewish victory in the secret report sent out by the Polish underground to London: "The German divisions that entered Ghetto territory at daybreak on April 19 were 'greeted'

---

[1] The matter of "Polish bandits" will be explained later.

by substantial and effective fire from the Ghetto fighters. The resistance was so strong that the Germans were forced to introduce ever new detachments into the battle, with field artillery, flame throwers, and tanks."

Now a Jewish source that portrays somewhat the German defeat: "The Jewish fighters 'greet' the Germans with a hail of grenades, bottles, bombs, and rifle shots. The only machine gun did not err. Nazi outlaws took off." (From the memoirs of group commander Hersz Berlinski, written in hiding on the Aryan side.)

How did the early battles on April 19, 1943, turn out?

Course of the First Battle at the Corner of Nalewki and Gesia

Two fighting groups under the command of Zekhariah Artszteyn and Leyb Rotblat occupied positions in corner houses at Nalewki 31 and Gesia 2; Nalewki 25, 27, 33, and 35, and in the house across the way at the intersection of Nalewki and Franciszkanska. The fighting group of Henryk Zylberberg fortified itself in the attic over the factory of Breuer, a German. Thus, the fighters intended to trap the invading Germans in a crossfire. Jewish armament consisted mainly of Molotov cocktails and grenades; they also had several pistols, rifles, and light machine guns. The fighters lurked at windows, balconies, and attics.

As German columns, singing heartily, moved into the intersection of Nalewki, Gesia, and Franciszkanska streets, they were suddenly barraged by Molotov cocktails, grenades, bombs, and bullets. The first shots came from the house at Nalewki 33, followed immediately by all other stations. The Germans were hit so suddenly that they fled in panic, leaving their dead and wounded on the pavement. When soon after they attempted to retrieve their casualties, they could not—so strong was the fire from Jewish positions. Soon, the rebels jumped out of their hiding places and took to shooting at the Nazis with pistols.

Great enthusiasm was aroused in the Jews by Germans fleeing at the first confrontation. The lusty song of SS men turned into cries of pain from their wounded. Tamar, a fighter, cried out, "This time they've paid!"

Soon the German officers reestablished control in their ranks. Von Sammern's staff was alerted and aid quickly came. The newly arrived soldiers did not dare advance openly, but they began chaotic shooting in the direction of the houses from which shots had earlier originated. Once more the two sides locked in battle. Once more the Jews not only held out, but also forced a second German retreat.

The initial battle on the corner of Nalewki and Gesia lasted two hours, from 6:00 to 8:00 A.M. Only the German side suffered. Thanks to their convenient positions the rebels lost not one person.

When the Nazi columns completely emptied out, the rebels came out of their hiding places and threw up their arms and congratulated one another. Then they pulled uniforms, helmets, and arms off the Nazi corpses that lay in the street.

Trap at Zamenhofa and Mila

Not much later a second skirmish broke out on the major Ghetto artery, somewhat more to the north, at the intersection of Zamenhofa and Mila.

Four fighting groups lay in wait for the enemy from four sides—groups led by Berl Broide, Aaron Briskin, Mordekhai Growas, and Levi Grozalc. They planned to catch the enemy there.

The rebels let the enemy "vanguard"—the Latvians and Jewish police—pass by. Only as the columns of Germans and Ukrainian Fascists appeared did the storm begin. By prearranged signal, a hail of grenades and rifle shots descended upon the enemy. Both in this attack and with their barrage of Molotov cocktails the rebels enjoyed unusual success. The Germans and Ukrainians offered no resistance and began running helter-skelter for cover among gateways or the open, blown-up stores.

Giving priority to saving their own skins, the Germans pushed the Ukrainians out of the gateways, and a quarter-hour passed before the officers could reassume control of the situation. The SS were first to return to the streets from hiding, and their officers, enraged and unnerved themselves, sought to drive the Ukrainians back to arms with whips. Equilibrium, though, had been destroyed. The enemy was rendered impotent because the Jews began a new, concentrated fire.

At that point the German command brought tanks into the Ghetto. The terrified Nazis moved forward behind these agents of destruction. Yet soon as the first tank reached the Mila–Zamenhofa intersection, it was bombarded with Molotov cocktails that found the mark and set it afire. The Jewish Fighting Organization report describes this unusual scene:

> The quiet, well–aimed throw of the bottle hits the tank; the flame spreads unusually fast. The blast of the explosion is heard; the machine is immobilized, its occupants burned alive. The next two tanks turn back and after them, in panic, flee the Germans who had hidden behind. We greet them with accurate shots and grenades.

After a brief interruption a fresh tank appeared; the rebels hurled a bomb at it. Again a German tank burned in Jewish streets. The enthusiasm of both Jewish combatants and civilians was enormous; their metamorphosis was unbelievable. An eyewitness writes:

> Yesterday's downtrodden, terrorized faces now show a joy so strange; inexpressible by words. A joy free of idiosyncracy, one stemming only from a sense of pride that the Ghetto fights back.

A second observer describes the Germans' retreat:

> There goes as if deranged a German soldier, with burning helmet on his head, making horrible noises. A second, as though possessed, yells "Jews . . . weapons. Jews . . . weapons."

Found among the wounded were two Ghetto police officers: Capt. Fleishman and Couns. Felz. The former was hated even by Ghetto police, four of whom he had sent to Auschwitz. The latter died of his wounds.

The dismal failure of von Sammern's troops at the Zamenhofa–Mila intersection was noted by Stroop in the report to his superior.

The tank and two armored cars used in the action were barraged with "Molotov cocktails." The tank caught fire twice. The attack led to the retreat of our fighting units. Losses in the initial assault: 12 (6 SS men and 6 Trawniki men [2]).

Losses among Jewish fighters in that battle were immeasurably smaller. At least one, Yekhiel, mentioned in Anielewicz's April 23 letter, fell.

The skirmish at the corner of Zamenhofa and Gesia lasted in all, one half-hour.

"All is Lost in the Ghetto!"

The officer in charge of the Nazi action, von Sammern, became completely baffled. He never dreamed of so strong a reaction from the Jewish "subhumans." Uncertain how to proceed, he desperately made his way to the Hotel Bristol at 7:30 A.M., where Himmler's emissary, Gen. Stroop, was quartered. The latter had arrived the day before to take control of Ghetto liquidation.

Stroop was still grooming himself as von Sammern burst in, yelling "All is lost in the Ghetto! We're no longer in the Ghetto! There's no way to get in there! We've got wounded and dead!"

Von Sammern maintained that the only solution was to bring in bombers from Cracow. However, Stroop did not advocate such compromising means, which would reveal German shame to the world. He immediately relieved the hapless SS and police chief of command of the Ghetto campaign and took over himself. He decided to penetrate the Ghetto, even at the great cost sure to result from so difficult a task. As he later explained in his own words, "Entry through Mila, Zamenhofa, Muranowska, or Nalewki was impossible because these streets were under steady fire [from the Jews]."

---

[2] "Trawniki men" refers to Ukrainian Fascists, German ethnics, and other collaborators who "studied" in the SS-training camp at Trawniki.

Second Battle at Nalewki and Gesia

After assuming command, Stroop introduced iron-handed discipline into his ranks and decided to alter von Sammern's plan. The latter had treated the assault on the Ghetto as an ordinary action, wanting to occupy the entire area with one sweep. As opposed to this, Stroop, acknowledging strong Jewish resistance at various points, decided to concentrate attack at one spot at a time. After conquering the first objective, he would attack a second, and a third, then drive the Jewish fighters into a pincer.

He soon had to modify his own plan because he had not accounted for the schemes and determination of his opponent.

At noon, Stroop reined in his troops and had them storm rebel positions at the Nalewki–Gesia intersection. Educated by the bitterness of that morning's skirmish, the Germans this time did not march parade fashion, but spread out and moved hugging the walls. The present assault was conducted—as on a regular battlefield —under cover of artillery fire. Gen. Stroop, the experience of two wars behind him—World War I on the French front and the World War II on the Soviet—placed light field artillery on Muranowski Square, and bombarded Jewish positions on Nalewki Street incessantly.

The Jewish fighters bravely defended themselves with grenades and Molotov cocktails, but light ammunition could not in any case stand up to cannon. The defense began to falter. Under such conditions, it is very difficult to hold a position, but the rebels held tenaciously, passing over roofs from house to house, all the while peppering the pursuing enemy with grenades.

At last Stroop brought in planes, which finally drove the Jews from the bombarded houses. Using up their Molotov cocktails and grenades, they retreated towards the tiny alleyway called Berish Majzels, taking with them the bodies of fallen comrades—among them the group leader, Zylberberg, and the fighter Tamar, who had so joyfully expressed her enthusiasm over the German defeat in the first confrontation.

Beginning at 6:00 A.M., armed resistance at Nalewki–Gesia positions lasted a total of six hours, without interruption.

Before retreating, the fighters set fire to the huge German warehouse at Nalewki 31. The Jewish Fighting Organization leadership had issued a command to burn all valuables and storehouses so nothing useful would be left to the enemy. This first large-scale act of sabotage served as signal for other arson. An observer from the Polish underground press made the following remark: "The Jews perish, weapons in hand, after first destroying valuable warehouses and burning factories."

The Nazi Murderers' Bloody Revenge

Enraged by the Jewish rebellion, Stroop's troops took immediate revenge that first day on the most innocent of the Jews, patients of the Ghetto hospital at Gesia 6. The hospital was situated in that portion of the street that lay outside the battle zone, and some of its nurses had brought aid to the rebels, carrying water or bandaging wounds. Nurses Blimberg and Rochman showed especial dedication in this respect.

The Germans vented their rage upon the sick, bombing and setting fire to the hospital while its helpless patients lay inside. In the yet undestroyed halls they carried out a horrible massacre, seizing patients and throwing them into the flames. They snatched infants and dashed their heads against the walls. In the delivery room, they bayoneted the bellies of women in childbirth.

The majority of hospital personnel perished in the flames. The Ukrainian Fascists especially distinguished themselves during the massacre by their sadism, to the great pleasure of their German masters. This was the mere beginning of the horrible murders that would continue until the end of the liquidation campaign against Ghetto resistance.

Clash on Muranowska Street

At 4:00 P.M., a large contingent of Nazis comprised of SS men and German police penetrated Muranowski Square and began shooting up Jewish homes. In reply, Farband contingents, holed up in the residential block extending from 7–21 Muranowska Street, opened heavy fire upon the invaders. Leading this defense were David Apelboim, Pawel Frenkl, and Leyb Rodal. They applied the tactic of attacking from several different points as they dashed from one spot to the next, throwing the Germans into total disarray. From then on, Jewish resistance grew increasingly strong. Stroop offers a description of the skirmish in his report:

> About 5:30 strong resistance was met at a certain housing complex from which [the Jews] were able to defend themselves with, among other items, machine guns. A special combat group [of Germans] drove out the enemy and entered the houses but took no captives. The Jews and outlaws defended themselves, going from one place to the other and finally disappeared over the roofs or through underground passages.

The strongest Jewish defense came from the battle station at Muranowska 7. On the roof of that building was a heavy machine gun that kept up continual fire against the Germans until 8:00 P.M. That position, as Stroop later admitted, dominated the entire Muranowski Square. Also Jewish warriors—men and women—moved over rooftops with uncanny agility as they hurled grenades at the Germans. Two resistance flags still waved over the house at Muranowska 7 when Stroop interrupted the battle in the evening. The Nazis did not conquer the Jewish stronghold on Muranowska that day.

Meanwhile, skirmishes on a smaller scale took place April 19, on Bonifraterska, Sapiezynska, Lubecki, and Stawki streets.

Governor General Frank's Urgent Letter to Berlin

The first day of Jewish rebellion has been inscribed in golden letters in the chronicles of the resistance movement. Jewish "sub-humans" took upon themselves the unequal struggle for their honor and freedom, chasing the arrogant "supermen" from the battlefield in disgrace.

The following day, April 20, Governor General of Poland Hans Frank dispatched an urgent letter to Reichsminister Dr. Lammers, chief of Hitler's chancellery in Berlin. It reads: "Since yesterday, we have in Warsaw a well-organized resistance in the Ghetto, which we must combat with artillery."

Marysia's Diary

While all this was occurring, in a Ghetto bunker a young girl sat entering her impression of the extraordinary events into her diary. She is known to us only by her signature (Marysia).

Yesterday [April 19] a truly bloody battle erupted in the Ghetto. Tanks, cannon, and heavy machine guns were moved into the Ghetto, and unmerciful war was declared upon the Jews who dared to raise their heads a bit in return for Treblinka, Belzec, Trawniki, and for the entire hell we live through.[3]

Indeed, the Ghetto prisoners perceived their struggle as Marysia described it in her diary. They saw in their fight not only the defense of dignity and life, but also a reply to all the misery Nazism had brought—to genocide.

---

[3] This diary was found in Majdanek where the author had been shipped and probably perished.

Seder in a Bunker

Night fell. Stroop pulled his troops out of the Ghetto. At resistance headquarters the situation was evaluated and plans were made for the next moves in the fighting. Reconnaissance groups surveyed the area. Now and then fighters struck up a song about their Ghetto-state; everywhere one felt pride mixed with anxiety. That night, as soon as shooting abated, traditional Jews sat down to the Seder in their bunkers.

One eyewitness, Ghetto fighter Simkha Korngold, portrayed the Seder of April 19, 1943, in the bunker at Karmelicka 5:

Five men stand watch outside with weapons in hand. My father sits in the bunker conducting the Seder. Two candles illuminate the cups of wine. To us, it appears the cups are filled with blood. All of us who sit here are the sacrifice. When "pour out your wrath" is recited we all shudder. We've awaited a miracle, but none appears.

3

The Second Day: April 20

German Ultimatum Rejected

The events of April 19 shook up the German military elite in Warsaw and elsewhere. Nazi military men passing through Warsaw from the eastern front on their way to Germany came to feel shame, not only for an obvious defeat but also over the folly of opening a front in the hinterlands, in the middle of a large city. Thus, with Warsaw serving as artery to the eastern front for soldiers and munitions, everyone knew that the blitzkrieg had failed also on the Ghetto front.

Hitler's officers took solace in the illusion that the Jews would not be able to maintain their superhuman efforts of the first day. The Germans began the second day's action with an ultimatum, apparently delivered by arrested members of the *Judenrat* presidium, demanding surrender in exchange for the "supermen's" mercy. The alternative was razing the Ghetto.

The ultimatum was rejected. Mordekhai Anielewicz later wrote of this on April 26, in a secret letter to Itzhak Cukierman on the Aryan side: "We've rejected the German ultimatum demanding capitulation."

The fight continued, and on Tuesday, April 20, was even extended to new parts of the Ghetto. For the first time the Germans were assaulted not only in the Central Ghetto but also in the brush factory sector, Swientojerska and Walowa streets, and the shop district, on Leszno, Smocza, and Nowolipie streets.

Also on the second day, the rebels had to face additional artillery set up just outside Ghetto walls at Krasinski Square and on Nowiniarska and Bonifraterska streets.

The Second Muranowska Street Battle

The first item on Stroop's agenda for Tuesday was the unfinished business from the day before: eradicating the rebel bastion on Muranowska Street. Two houses in that sector, numbers 7 and 9, still held out, and on the roof of number 7 two bullet-riddled flags fluttered proudly the morning of April 20, one white and red and the other white and blue.

The second Muranowska Street battle would prove to be very fierce. Early that morning German police, packed in tens of autos, encircled the block containing numbers 7 and 9. They opened fire upon the two buildings and hurled grenades through the windows. The rebels inside were supposed to panic; instead those in number 7 responded with machine-gun fire. A number of German policemen were either killed or wounded and the others panicked and ran away. This caused a half-hour interruption in the fighting until the German command brought in five small tanks equipped with anti-aircraft artillery.

The Jews, concealed behind windows and in attics, bombarded the tanks with machine-gun fire. They stopped one dead in its tracks with a grenade; the other tanks had taken positions 50 meters away, out of range of rebel fire. German tank guns then began a terrible bombardment of Jewish houses. Grenades were hurled back from the latter but fell short of the mark and caused no damage.

Within a quarter-hour this unequal confrontation left most of the area buildings in ruins, and against the weakening resistance the Germans mustered enough courage to enter the badly damaged houses with machine guns and grenades. A brief hand-to-hand skirmish ensued in which a rebel group surrendered when its ammunition ran out. Relying upon a written account by an eyewitness, M. Berland, we can get a sense of what the terrorized Jewish civilians saw from their hiding places.

The Germans rounded up a group of eighty fighters, mainly youths, and surrounded them with a guard of three hundred soldiers, ready to shoot. The prisoners were bleeding, many with head or foot wounds or partially severed hands, their clothes stained and tattered, but their faces betrayed neither fear nor defeat. Indeed, they showed elation in having repaid the Germans to some extent. They were proud to have carried out their duty while recognizing that ahead of them lay only death.

Here is a hymn of praise to the soldiers of Muranowska composed by an eyewitness, known to us only by the name Shlomo:

> When at Passover time we were ordered to abandon the Ghetto, our boys and girls, our unknown soldiers, offered fitting resistance. Their motto was "Live or die, let my soul perish among the Philistines!" Thousands of young men and women, armed with revolvers, grenades, machine guns, and bombs resisted the murderers. Hundreds of SS men died and our youth was pleased to leave this world having killed the murderers.
>
> I am the man who has seen all!

As evidenced by his report, Tuesday's combat would remain in Stroop's memory, especially the fight over the flags and the loss of SS Cavalry Lt. Otto Demke. For Demke, the first enemy officer killed by the Jews in the Uprising, Stroop took bloody revenge; several hundred Jews were executed on the spot. The shooting was carried out by Dr. Hahn's Security Police division under supervision of Witosek, a notorious Nazi murderer. By Stroop's order, the flags were captured and taken to police headquarters where they became trophies of the battle.

In Coffins to Otwock

Not all Muranowska combatants fell into the hands of the Germans. Most of them broke through to a tunnel and, with the help of the combined Polish–Jewish group of Maj. Iwanski, reached the Otwock railway line.[1] There, their guide, Marian Kowalski ("Semp") placed them in coffins procured from a Christian funeral home in Wolia, a working-class district. The coffins also contained rifles, machine guns, and grenades. Commanded by Leyb Rodal, the goal of these ex-prisoners and their guide was to reach the forest and organize a partisan camp.

The group settled in an abandoned villa in the woods between Michalin and Jozefow. Two days later, on April 22, the villa was surrounded by German and Polish police, the way having been pointed out by a local police official. With the Jews unwilling to surrender, a tragic battle broke out in the middle of the pine forest. The Jews, wounded and weakened from the struggle in the Ghetto, still fought with great determination, but were finally forced to attempt escape by running deeper into the forest. To stay in the villa would have meant being burned alive. This effort failed and all were seized and killed, including the commander, Leyb Rodal. An official report by the Otwock gendarmerie was issued April 23.

Back on Muranowska Street, a third combat group of seven members had found a hiding place and remained there from Tuesday till the following day, April 21. At that time, taking their arms and ammunition, they passed through a tunnel to a house at Muranowska 6 and hid there in the attic, waiting for someone from Iwanski's group to lead them to the forest. The watchman there, a Christian, was trusted by the Jews, but his son turned out to be a scoundrel, a member of the fascist group Miecz i Plug and a Gestapo confidant. His name was Andrzej Michno, but he was called Ryszek. This creature did not hesitate to betray his own father and immediately summoned the Gestapo and Polish police who surrounded the house and slaughtered all the Jewish fighters.

[1] Otwock was a resort town not far from Warsaw—*trans.*

A fourth fighting squad under David Apelboim—all four belonged to the Farband—was still hiding at Muranowska 7 and decided to remain there and gather strength for coming struggles. Other Farband members under Pawel Frenkl who had been fighting at Muranowska fled to the Aryan side. There some stayed in the city and others proceeded to Otwock where they assaulted Polish police and liberated several arrested girls. Then they continued deeper into the woods, after which all trace of them was lost.

Mine Explosion in the Brush Factory Area

In the brush factory area Jewish fighting groups applied a tactic similar to that in the Central Ghetto. This defense sector comprised ten houses on 28–38 Swientojerska Street that faced the Aryan side, and several neighboring houses on Walowa Street. Specifically, defense of the brush factory area consisted of placing a mine under the little square at the gateway to Walowa 6. On the third floor of Walowa 3 an observation point was set up from which the square in front of number 6 could easily be observed. An area weapons and ammunition arsenal was set up in Farband member Szymon Katz's bunker.

Led by their chief and co-commander for the battle, Police Maj. Oskar Zigenis, Stroop's forces began an attack on the area Tuesday, April 20, at 3:00 P.M. Having heard that Stroop was to become the victim of assassination—at least this is what he claimed after the war at his Warsaw trial—his men provided him, like an African chieftain of old, with a protective umbrella—two SS soldiers holding loaded automatic rifles over his head.

At his trial five years later, Stroop would recall the first brush factory confrontation as a particularly heavy one. Three hundred of Hitler's soldiers and officers stormed the factory area fortress. The Jews allowed them to reach the gate at Walowa 6, where they stepped on the fuse and exploded the mine. "Stones, clods of earth, and torn limbs from bodies of SS men ended up in a mishmash," a Fighting Organization report reads. Twenty-two Nazis fell dead on the spot.

The Germans panicked. The three hundred once-splendidly arrayed soldiers ran amok, tripping over one another trying to flee the inferno of bullets and grenades exploding all about them. The "superman" cried out in German: "Yes, the Jews did it!"—their exclamations mixed with the screams of the wounded who were left lying unprotected on the pavement. After a brief staff consultation, a well-covered group of Germans returned with stretchers to remove their casualties. For more than an hour all stayed quiet and the insurgents, led by Marek Edelman, took the opportunity to refortify their positions.

The Germans soon commenced a new assault, this time not by mass invasion, but cautiously, two-by-two, along the walls. Greeted with grenades, Molotov cocktails, and two heavy bombs, the Germans again retreated—and again the air was rent by the screams of the gravely wounded. Stroop ordered his men to unleash a continual, heavy rain of bullets; this time the Jewish reply was not so strong; ammunition was running low. The Jewish commander forbade bullets to be fired except into a group of Germans; every bullet was precious.

Suddenly the unbelievable: Nazi shooting ceased and several men with white flags moved toward the Jewish stronghold. The Jews recognized the leader of this delegation, the German factory director, Lautz. By sending negotiators, the Nazi command had apparently decided to treat the Jews like a legitimate military opponent rather than as "bandits," "creatures," and "subhumans"—terms used in Stroop's reports. Lautz proposed a quarter-hour ceasefire for removal of the dead and for the Jews to leave their hiding places.

The proposal was rejected with disgust; deals are not made with mass murderers, especially when they continue their evil during negotiations. In this case, SS men were setting fire to buildings in a different area. Only a few mentally broken victims heeded the Nazi order to relinquish their shelter.

Stroop responded to the rejection with overwhelming artillery bombardment. "The 10 mm. howitzers thrown into battle chased the bands from their strongholds," he wrote in his report of April 20.

He did not stop the fighting until nightfall. Then the rebels took stock of their situation and decided to move on to a new position in

nearby Franciszkanska Street. The retreat, made difficult by om-
nipresent enemy searchlights, was covered by Jurek Blones's squad.
One of his fighters succeeded in putting a light out of service with a
well-aimed bullet.

In that day's battles in the brush factory area many Jewish
fighters distinguished themselves by their bravery and contempt for
death. Among those who perished heroically were Renja Niemiecka,
a young fighter in Jurek Grynszpan's group, and Michal Klepfisz, an
engineer, who died at his post, gun in hand. His comrades buried
him at 4:00 A.M. in a little garden in the courtyard of Swientojerska
34.

During the night retreat to Franciszkanska Street, Berek
Szneidman, a fighter and secretary of the Jewish Labor Bund, was
killed, as was Jacob Praszker and his friend Rosza Mastboim, both
of whom had already reached safety on Franciszkanska but returned
to bring back others.

A survivor, forty-year-old Abraham Diament, an ex-sergeant of
the Polish army, who had killed six Germans, was one of the oldest
rebels. Some of the younger, like Szagan Lent, Luszek Blones, and
Szlamek Szuster, also distinguished themselves by being among the
best marksmen. Such fighters showed not only bravery but also
tremendous agility in shooting at the enemy from rooftops and from
behind chimneys. "A Jew lay on a roof behind a chimney and fired
at the Germans," a Polish report read. A leftist Polish underground
newspaper "Gwardzista" was justified in writing: "At the brush
district on Swientojerska and Franciszkanska battles were particularly severe. One fighting group held a certain portion of the
street a whole day without allowing one enemy detachment to pass."

Another underground publication, "Robotnik," wrote: "The
brush factory workers carried out a concentrated counterattack."

Ambush by Jewish Fighters on Berish Majzels Street

Approximately the same time another battle was taking
place—this time on Berish Majzels Street. The Germans changed the
name of this little backdoor corridor between Nalewki and Zamen-

hofa streets to Kurza (Chicken) Street, as they had changed the name Zamenhofa back to Dzika. The Fighting Organization command had not accounted for Majzels Street in the battle plan, but on April 20, this territory was to become by chance the arena of a brief rebel triumph. Such achievements attest to the excellent rebel awareness of the terrain plus marvelous resourcefulness in exploiting that knowledge. Two participants in this skirmish, Chaim Frimer and Tuvia Borzykowski, gave this brief account of their experience:

> By chance we found ourselves on Huener Street and sensing that the Germans were in pursuit we decided to trap them in a crossfire. They paid with several dead. We got away unharmed and ran off toward Mila Street where fighting had been going on for several days.

Red Flag Over Mila—Death Leap Through Fire

Mila Street, home of the Jewish proletariat and the poor, was now the center of Jewish resistance. It lay under the control of the rebels, whose general staff was headquartered there amidst a large network of underground bunkers and Fighting Organization arsenals. Atop one of the tallest buildings the rebels mounted a red flag, the object of Stroop's April 20 attack on the area. The general gave much energy to this task, and he would succeed to boast of his trophy to another SS bigwig, Odilo Globocnik of Lublin.

The Germans commenced the assault on Mila the same afternoon as the attack on the brush factory area, but here they found no single concentrated Jewish position; instead there were several pockets of resistance. Unfortunately we have no precise description of the events of the battle and they appear to have been quite confusing.

Here is a picture of one incident. A youth lay on a rooftop, firing a machine gun at the Germans until his ammunition ran out. He was hit by an enemy bullet and fell dead in front of his gun. At the same time the Germans were driving a group of helpless Jews to the *Umschlagplatz* and came under fire from a combat squad. Upon reaching the corner of Zamenhofa and Mila, the Germans fled, shooting at their prisoners, who scattered in all directions.

Mila 5 was the scene of a tragic struggle. The Germans surrounded the house and ordered all Jews to leave. When they refused, the Germans bombarded the building, leaving it in flames. The inhabitants, faced by flames on one side and Germans on the other, ran into the courtyard where they gathered around some fighters they trusted would find a way out. The only solution was to leap through the flames and the gateway while shooting at the enemy. The fighters moved first, followed by the entire mass of people. They reached the other side of the flames, and the Germans—apparently unready to do combat with those willing to risk all—were no longer there. Nevertheless, for their escape the Jews paid dearly in singed hair, faces, and clothes, and with wounds on their hands and feet.

Initial Battles at Leszno, Nowolipie, and Smocza Streets

The aforementioned four confrontations all took place within a relatively limited area; the fifth sector, further removed from the others included the even-numbered side of Leszno (divided from the odd side by the Ghetto wall), Nowolipie, Nowolipki, and Smocza streets.

In the latter sector Toebbens and Schultz, the German factory owners and SS intimates, still tried to maintain control and induce Jewish laborers and office employees to report for deportation. Their line was the cynical contention that the shooting and fighting going on in other parts of the Ghetto were just the work of bandits, ungrateful to the Germans whose only concern was the welfare of the Jews.

Assuring Stroop that they could take care of the Jews themselves, Toebbens and Schultz requested that no troops be sent to their factories. Aiding the bosses were Jewish traitors—factory supervisors or partners of the owners—who urged the Jews to give themselves up voluntarily. Generally such appeals were ignored; the Jews preferred hiding or else sabotaging German orders.

Thus, since the shops had not been touched by invading Nazi

troops, when the rebels began battling in the area their act was one of offense, not defense. They wanted to come to the aid of comrades in the other sectors by attacking the columns of German detachments passing through Leszno and Smocza on the way to Nalewki and Zamenhofa.

The main positions of the Jewish Fighting Organization were in buildings at Leszno 36, 72, 74, and 76; Nowolipie 31, 41, 66, and 67, and Smocza 4–10. At 6:00 A.M. on Tuesday, with tanks in the lead, an enemy formation of soldiers singing a gay military tune to the accompaniment of a marching band stepped through the odd-numbered Aryan side of Leszno. Suddenly, from rebel stations on the other side of the Ghetto wall in Leszno 74 and 76 came a barrage of pistol and rifle shots, Molotov cocktails and grenades, plus two bombs. Instantly the other Jewish positions on Leszno joined in and eight Germans fell to the pavement.

This heroic attack by Jewish rebels deeply impressed the democratic Polish underground press. "Gwardzista" of April 20 reports: "The Hitlerite detachments marching through the territory of Toebbens and Schultz were attacked with grenades and gunfire." The same day, a bulletin of the Polish underground council to aid Jews reads: "In the early morning hours hand grenades unexpectedly fell upon the SS detachment marching through Leszno. The Jews were on the offensive."

A Jewish eyewitness survivor of that action, Felix Olar, verifies the heroic stance of those Jewish fighters:

> From the front windows came a hail of grenades, and from the other side of the street, the moans and groans of wounded soldiers. Then a gun battle ensued, our people shooting from windows, theirs from the street. Our side fought in every possible way. The girls brought grenades. I looked at their calm faces, faces without tears or fear. They were ready to die honorably on the spot. Never will I forget those faces.

Rivka Feker, a courier acting on behalf of Eliezer Geller, military staff liaison in the shop district, immediately delivered a report of the above incidents to Mila headquarters.

Soon there was more action on Smocza near Nowolipie. Expecting a second SS column to pass this way to the Central Ghetto, the Smocza insurgents placed a mine under the pavement. Unfortunately there was no explosion and the enemy proceeded safely. The rebels, undismayed, immediately pelted a tank with Molotov cocktails, setting it aflame.

Dorka Goldkorn, a young rebel fighter, was in the Smocza sector at the time and describes her reaction as they watched the burning tank: "We jumped for joy as we saw the tank in flames. That was the most beautiful moment of our lives; afterward there were no more such happy moments."

Stroop then ordered an all-out assault on rebel positions in Leszno and Smocza streets, forcing his opponent to abandon Leszno and retreat to Nowolipie. His men took revenge by destroying dwellings and bunkers, driving their occupants into the street and shooting many on the spot.

Many rebels, known and unknown, distinguished themselves in the fighting at Leszno and Smocza. Among the former were Eliezer Geller and Rivka Szmutka, the first ones to hurl grenades and bombs at the Germans. Among the anonymous were heroes who displayed great ingenuity coupled with tremendous courage. One report relates the following incident:

> A young Jew, hands over his head, ran out of a gateway and cried out to the Germans: "Smocza 5 gives up!" The Germans moved toward the gate, and as they came close those inside Smocza 5 greeted them with heavy fire. The self-sacrificing young fighter was killed by the Germans, but they in turn paid a heavy price.

The fighters on Smocza and Leszno suffered grave losses. On April 20, in one station alone, twenty of fifty-six young Jewish men and women perished. On that day the Germans were attacked from still another point.

Solidarity Action by People's Guard on Nowiniarska Street

As soon as the first Jewish shots were heard in the Ghetto on April 19, a secret meeting of the Warsaw leadership of the leftist guerrilla group, the People's Guard, was held on Brisk Street in Praga, just outside the city. There it was decided to attack the German artillery battery on Nowiniarska Street that was bombarding battle stations in the brush factory area of the Ghetto. The People's Guard, at that time still small in numbers and poor in supplies, realized it was strong enough only to contribute isolated acts of solidarity, like stilling the German artillery on Nowiniarska.

Participating in this action was a special squad of the Warsaw People's Guard named for Ludwig Warynski. Members included the artists Franciszek Bartoszek (commander) and Sigmund Bobowski; Jerzy Duracz, son of Theodore Duracz, famous political lawyer; and Niuta Teitelboim, a heroic Jewish warrior and Ghetto liaison officer. Their attack, undertaken April 20 at 7:00 P.M., was a complete success. In full view of a largely German mob, and without a single loss of their own, squad members destroyed the enemy battery crew—two German artillerymen and two Polish policemen.

The same day a second People's Guard group of four Poles and their leader Lerski (pseudonym for Lerner, a Jew) assaulted a patrol of SS men and Polish police at the intersection of Gesia and Okopowa streets. This effort was only partially successful.

Solidarity Action of Land Army Youth in Sapiezynska

On April 19 a secret meeting was also held by the high command of the so-called Land Army (A.K.) that was responsible to the Sikorski government-in-exile in London. The session was not called specifically to discuss the Ghetto Uprising. Commander-in-chief "Grot" (Stefan Rowecki) was not present and was represented by Gen. "Bor" (Komorowski), who was part of the anti-Semitic "Endek" group.

The commander of A.K.'s Warsaw region, "Monter" (Antony Chruszczel) astonished Gen. Bor by his declaration of readiness to offer aid to the Ghetto fighters. Indeed, Monter, whose political orientation was close to that of Polish democratic circles, had already ordered a resistance action behind Ghetto walls. The action took place unsuccessfully that same day at 7:00 P.M., with the participation of a sizable A.K. group of young workers and students from the Targowek suburb. Led by Maj. "Chwatski" (Jozef Pszenny), the group was to blow up a segment of the Ghetto wall on Sapiezynska Street to enable a number of Jews to break out and flee in the direction of the Zoliborz region. The action was frustrated when Polish police spotted the A.K. soldiers and alerted the Germans, who fired heavily upon them. In the ensuing skirmish two Germans and two Polish policemen were killed, also two A.K. members, Eugenius Morawski and Jozef Wilk. Two other Poles suffered heavy wounds, and others, minor injuries. Protected by darkness, the Land Army group retreated with its dead and wounded.

Yankel Rakower and Friends Break Out of the Ghetto

It appears that the plans of Maj. Chwatski's group were known to one of the paramilitary porter groups on Mila and Wolynska streets. The group's leader, Yankel Rakower, a porter, decided to seize the opportunity to flee the Ghetto. Although Chwatski's efforts did not succeed, Rakower's did. He and a dozen armed porters made their way through the Jewish cemetery west of Okopowa Street and managed to escape to Zoliborz. There they joined a partisan detachment of the 4th Brigade of the Polish People's Army (P.A.L.) apparently headed for the Kampinos woods. They were never heard from again.

4

Battles Within the Burning Walls:
April 21–26

Fresh Fighting on Leszno

Confident after the events of the previous day that the Jews would submit without resistance to deportation, Stroop concentrated his main forces around Schultz's factory on Leszno Street at dawn of Wednesday, April 21. At 7:00 A.M., Schultz summoned the Jews to a meeting in the factory yard. Using soft talk interspersed with threats, the entrepreneur posed an ultimatum: either go willingly to Poniatow or the troops would be admitted for a pogrom.

"Swindler! You want to drive us to our death! Give back our wives and children!" the mob, menacing, screamed. Schultz disappeared immediately, the military entered, and the Jews ran off. Suddenly, Jewish grenades rained down upon the Germans, leaving four of them lying in a pool of blood.

The massacre began. SS men and their Ukrainian–Latvian underlings hurled grenades, blew up bunkers, shot and slaughtered. The Jewish combat groups that had either returned from Smocza Street or had not left the factory area the day before scampered to the higher stories of the factory buildings and fired at the Nazis. They were pursued by the latter and climbed even higher. When a fire broke out they escaped to adjoining buildings. The fighting group under David Nowodworski especially distinguished itself in that unequal confrontation. Meanwhile skirmishes erupted on Smocza and Nowolipie streets where Hersz Kawe and Adam Szwarcfus headed the defense. Szymon Heller, one of the Jewish Fighting Organization's best marksmen, emerged the battle's hero. He did not waste a bullet; each found its target.

In a day consisting mainly of defensive actions by bunker groups the rebellion spread to Zamenhofa, Nalewki, Mila, Niska, Szczeszliwa, Wolynska, Pokorna, Franciszkanska, Swientojerska, and Walowa streets. No bunker gave up without a fight. On April 21, Stroop reported "The enemy fought today with the same armaments as yesterday, but added specially prepared explosive materiel." (The explosives referred to were Molotov cocktails and probably a new type of mine.) At Zamenhofa 30, after a long defense action by a barricaded Jewish group, the Germans burned down the house. At Franciszkanska 36 and Walowa 4, combat groups firing at invading Nazis forced them into the courtyards.

Taking stock of that Wednesday's bloody action, Stroop wrote that 150 Jews fell in battle and another 80 in demolished bunkers. He acknowledged the Jews fought heroically, especially women, whom he believed to be members of the "Jewish Pioneer Movement Women's Combat Organization." The entire day bombs fell upon Jewish buildings from ground and air. Stroop's planes dropped leaflets urging capitulation together with loads of explosives and incendiary bombs.

The Ghetto had become both battlefront and hell.

April 21, at Night

The Germans were under the impression that Jewish insurgents at Schultz's Leszno Street factory had already been "smoked out," yet by nightfall of April 21 they reappeared. The following account of that Wednesday night is based upon the testimony of eyewitness Itzhak Gitler, who later wrote his memoirs in hiding on the Aryan side.

By nightfall, the Jewish fighters were suddenly back on the roofs and in attics, observing movements of German night patrols and visiting bunkers where civilians were hiding. The fighters helped the latter relocate after their original shelters had been discovered by the enemy.

This was a rather odd undertaking. Protected by armed combatants, two long columns of people crept by dark along the rooftops. Light was provided by the burning houses. Old women were carried on the backs of their rescuers, who inched their way on all fours. They had to cross one roof to the next over boards or makeshift bridges.

The unique rescue was led by two daring, nimble young men, Jacob and Lolek, whose first names only were recalled by Gitler. Perhaps they were Jacob Feigenblat and Lev Rudnycki, group commanders in Gordonia (a Zionist youth organization) and the Polish Workers Party, respectively.

Thursday, April 22: Fresh Fighting on Leszno Street

The initiative of Jewish fighters on Leszno was immeasurable. After the previous night's dangerous expedition they cropped up again on Thursday morning, April 22, and once more frustrated the continuing Nazi attempts at pogrom and deportation.

The Germans and their henchmen commenced the morning action by blowing up the gates to Leszno houses with grenades. Then they penetrated the domiciles themselves and proceeded to demolish the bunkers there. Fighters hiding in the upper stories assaulted their enemy with rifle fire and grenades, but the latter had positioned themselves out of easy range of Jewish fire. From well-shielded emplacements the Germans in turn attacked the higher floors with grenade launchers. The rebels were helpless.

The Ghetto in Flames

That day Jews carried out similar acts of resistance in other sectors of the Ghetto front. At the same time, Stroop realized that he was subjecting his men to great sacrifice and decided to substitute fire for hand-to-hand clashes with the rebels. He ordered further burning of buildings. On April 22, a conflagration began in the Ghetto unknown since Nero set Rome aflame. This ghastly turn of events elicited the following communiqué from the Jewish Fighting Organization:

> Thursday passed under the omen of giant fires first on Swientojerska, Franciszkanska, Walowa, and Nalewki, and later on Zamenhofa Street. They had been ignited by demolition and incendiary bomb units of the German artillery. Clouds of smoke expanding with each passing hour hang over the entire Ghetto. The flames rage with indescribable force, and the streets are engulfed by thick, biting smoke. Realizing they could not break Jewish resistance by arms the Germans chose destruction by fire. Thousands of screaming women and children have been burned alive in dwellings. The victims appear through windows like living torches.

With sadistic delight Stroop emphasizes the results of his work in his April 22 report: "Whole Jewish families, swallowed by flames jumped en masse from windows or let themselves down by knotted sheets. Immediate attempt was made to liquidate both the former and the latter escapees."

The aforementioned Fighting Organization bulletin mentions nothing of events on Muranowska Street, but already by Thursday houses were burning there. Berland, an eyewitness, relates:

> Two men and a woman lean from a window. Disheveled, faces blackened, clothes burning on their bodies ... the "scene" being photographed by loudly laughing Germans. More and more persons run out of the fire, hurl themselves to the ground, writhe in pain as flames jump at them with no let up. No one quenches the flames or offers assistance. All that is heard is the mocking laughter of human devils. Finally the sated Germans line up and march off in song.

These same smug arsonists cravenly took to their heels when attacked by Jewish fighters. Although fire made the struggle more difficult, rebel mobility was clearly never broken. On the enflamed Swientojerska, Franciszkanska, Muranowska, and, of course,

Leszno, Jews assaulted Germans at every opportunity. That the situation of the latter had been made difficult is evidenced by Stroop's filing three reports for that Thursday.

That day Anielewicz sent a secret letter from the burning Ghetto to comrades on the Aryan side:

> We are all well. Have you sent food packages [read: weapons] yet? Don't forget eggs [grenades] and candy [bullets], and, of course, that which our aunt needs most [rifles]. Forget about the salami [revolvers]. We're trying to figure out how to get together with you. Let T. (Tuvia Szeingut, a courier) go to the cemetary to pray for the souls of the dead.

The last sentence means contact should be maintained through the cemetery.

Michalek's Heroic Act

During the Uprising many deeds of heroism shone forth—some already noted. The following feat was performed by one of the youngest rebels, Michalek. His real name was Henjek Kleinweiss.

Ghetto product, abandoned child, Michalek was one of the many such souls spawned by the streets. Before the Uprising he lived by selling lemonade in the streets and there made friends with the fighting youth. When rebellion was about to break out he joined the Jewish Fighting Organization and at once became a favorite of his comrades. Intelligent, courageous, agile, and eager, Michalek quickly mastered the use of arms. Assigned to the Leszno sector, he would assume and fulfill the most difficult tasks. Fear was foreign to him.

A crucial mission came his way: to escort Zionist youth activist Chana Platnyka from the rebel position on Leszno to the Aryan side. She was to travel to the Bedzin Ghetto in the name of the Fighting Organization to speed up preparations there for armed resistance.

The expedition failed. Platnyka, Michalek, and a third companion were seized by the Germans. They were to be executed or deported, but Michalek was destined to emerge a hero. Jacob Putermilch, a survivor who fought beside him, relates what happened.

While being led away Michalek suddenly told a German officer that he knew the whereabouts of a bunker with concealed Jews. His captors willingly followed his instructions. Upon entering the passageway to Leszno 74 the youth quickly pulled away the German officer's revolver and shot him dead. Before the other Germans in the convoy could collect their wits Michalek and his comrade disappeared; Platnyka, however, did not get far before getting killed by the Germans. Michalek suddenly reappeared, killed two more Germans and made off again, leaving the enemy to curse the arrogant youth who tricked them so dearly.

The price paid by the Jews was also overwhelming: Chana Platnyka was considered a gem among Jewish resistance fighters in Poland. Later Michalek also met his end. When the author of this book asked the mentioned Putermilch to name a particularly outstanding rebel fighter, he offered the name and story of Henjek Kleinweiss.

Battles Amid Flames: Friday, April 23

On April 23, Himmler dispatched an order through Krueger, higher SS and police chief in Cracow, to speed up the Ghetto "cleanup" with absolute severity. Stroop writes in his report: "I had therefore decided to raze the housing blocks in the Jewish residential district, plus those at the arms factories. One factory building after another was emptied and burned down." In the April 23 report Stroop assures his superiors, "The campaign will be completed today."

The general erred. That very Friday he was forced to admit, "The Jews and outlaws held out till the last moment, shooting at the attacking units." Fighting groups under Eliezer Geller, Benjamin Wald, Szymon Heller, David Nowodworski, and Hersz Kawe distinguished themselves in those assaults upon the Germans. After retreating from the residential area they reappeared on Leszno and Nowolipie streets to harass the enemy.

That day two announcements appeared on the Aryan side: one by Stroop, now the officially appointed SS and police chief of Warsaw in place of von Sammern; the other by the Jewish Fighting Organization. The former was legal, pasted on walls and posts throughout the city; the latter was illegal, secretly disseminated. Stroop's notice sentenced to death anyone entering the Ghetto without a permit. The Fighting Organization's appealed "to Poles, freedom fighters," that the battle is "for your liberation and ours" and would continue till the last breath. Its author was Itzhak Samsonowicz, Jewish Labor Bund activist, and it was distributed by Polish socialists and underground activists.

On April 23, in protest against the notice, the Polish resistance movement staged several solidarity actions for the Fighting Organization. A People's Guard squad under Dr. Henryk Sztenhel ("Gustav"), a onetime Spanish Civil War volunteer, attacked a motorized patrol on Ferta Street in the older part of the city in front of a home where Germans were searching for hidden Jews. The action succeeded. A German auto was burned and the four or five soldiers inside were killed. The squad suffered no loss and the intended captives were saved.

On Gesia, a second People's Guard group fell upon Germans, but this time the latter prevailed. Lerski (Lerner), a People's Guard commander, took his own life with a grenade to avoid capture. The same day two small groups consisting only of Land Army officers attacked Germans near the Jewish cemetery. These two moves, purely symbolic, were the end of A.K. solidarity actions on the Ghetto's behalf. Neither these nor earlier ones on April 20 were judged worth publicizing by A.K. leadership. On the other hand, the People's Guard issued bulletins of its efforts for the Ghetto and called upon other organizations to follow its example. There will be further accounts of its solidarity.

Bold Plan to Demolish Gestapo Headquarters

Their tragic situation did not break down the fighters, but rather inspired them to undertake actions far beyond their resources. Friday, April 23 was also the day a combat squad stationed at the Nowolipie–Karmelicka intersection concocted a truly fantastic plan: to blow up Gestapo headquarters at Zelazna 103—torture chamber for Jews and the residence of Brand, the hangman. This group, commanded by Natan Szule, had indeed set out for the target but was intercepted on the way by a strong German patrol. After a brief skirmish most of the Jewish fighters were killed; the enemy paid too with several dead and wounded.

Saturday, April 24: Jews Answer Fire with Fire

The Ghetto blazed on. *Wehrmacht* demolition teams moved through the streets dynamiting building after building. Planes circling continuously overhead dropped firebombs. Still the rebels held out. Their communiqué for the day read: "Struggling grimly the fighters continue to pound the enemy. They set fire to German weapons, factories, and arsenals."

April 24, first Sabbath of the insurrection, the rebels repaid fire with fire, destroying the huge Pfeiffer & Weigl tannery, army storehouses of woolen and other manufactures, and the military cannery. In his report Stroop admits that the Jews would rather perish by the conflagration than fall to the hands of the genocides. He added: "The Jews kept shooting until the action was over. By the end of the day a demolition team under machine-gun cover had to destroy a solid concrete house." Similar struggles took place on Mila, Bonifraterska, Muranowska, Leszno, Nowolipie, and Nowolipki streets.

In the latter three areas, by Saturday, a sizeable number of civilians had broken down and presented themselves for deportation. Informers cropped up who, brutalized by the Nazis, pointed out the locations of the bunkers. They denounced the rebels while trying to persuade other Jews to abandon their hiding places rather than succumb by flame.

Yet at Leszno 74, 76, 78; Nowolipie 67, 68; and Nowolipki 21 and 41 the fighters held their ground. Stroop visited that sector and marveled at persons battling from burning buildings. Actually, the combatants had moved to the rooftops and, from there, shot at the Germans below. When Stroop discovered these new positions he ordered his men to direct their fire accordingly. Then the Jews maneuvered from corner to corner, roof to roof, before the eyes of their Swastikaed hunters, and vanished from sight.

Evacuation from Mila's Doomed Bunkers

That Saturday brought great agony to Mila Street dwellers. Flames and explosions abounded; houses, and even bunkers, were made unsafe. The Jewish Fighting Organization decided to evacuate civilians to safer bunkers. In one such effort they removed inhabitants of the Mila 29 bunker to temporary quarters in a bunker at Mila 9. Armed with rifles, revolvers, and grenades, groups led by Aaron ("Pawel") Briskin and Leyb ("Lutek") Rotblat formed a fore and rear guard; in between, the crowd of civilians marched in exemplary order.

The same day the fighting group of Zekhariah Artszteyn carried out a rescue operation on Niska Street involving many Jews. At 6:00 P.M., after Germans had attacked the street and drenched houses with kerosene, Artszteyn's group opened fire on the invaders. The Jewish defenders had to retreat, but not before they artfully led civilians to safety through holes in the walls. During the action one fighter, Walsdorf, was lost.

Three days later a similar evacuation was conducted from Mila 37 to safer quarters at Mila 7 by squads under Levi Grozalc and David Hochberg. There, the latter died a hero's death. When the Germans suddenly fell upon the crowd, Hochberg blocked the narrow entrance with his body, thus saving the entire throng of Jews.

New Partisan Tactics

With the enemy destroying the Ghetto by fire, the rebel command was forced to change battle tactics. It decided to drop open warfare in favor of concealing forces underground and employing sudden guerrilla-type attacks and retreats. In an April 23 letter, Anielewicz informed comrades on the Aryan side of the change: "Beginning today, we adopt partisan tactics."

This consisted of forming groups of up to ten members dressed in German uniforms and helmets, their feet wrapped in rags to silence their steps as they left the bunkers by night for ambush, espionage, food and arms searches, and attacks on the rear flanks of enemy patrols. The first three such squads were dispatched by Anielewicz the night of April 23; later the number of expeditions increased. The first night the fighters assaulted patrols on Mila, Dzika, Szczeszliwa, Swientojerska, and Walowa streets.

Execution of the *Judenrat*

On Saturday, April 24, news reached the Ghetto that the Nazis had shot all four members of the *Judenrat* presidum: Marek Lichtenboim, Gamze Wielikowski, Alfred Sztolcman, and Stanislaw Szereszewski. They had been arrested as hostages at the beginning of the Ghetto liquidation. Next the Nazis did away with the Jewish Ghetto police. The last member was executed at Gestapo headquarters, Zelazna 103.

Tragic Losses: April 25

Sunday, April 25, the Jewish Fighting Organization suffered a grievous. loss. The rebel leaders had decided, for the first time, to send emissaries to the Aryan side to make contacts and explore possibilities for either a relief or a rescue operation. Trying to find a way there, the sentinels arranged for aid from fire fighters operating in the area of the burning Ghetto. (Forbidden to extinguish the fires, the firemen were charged with preventing their spread to the Aryan side.) The two groups were to meet on April 25, but the sentinels were detected in transit by an enemy patrol. In an unequal confrontation the Jewish contingent was destroyed, except for a critically wounded man who was barely able to crawl back to Fighting Organization headquarters.

The tragedy was double—the attempt to set up the desired contacts with the Aryan side was thwarted, while some of the most adroit Jewish fighters were lost in a fruitless action.

Intensified Fighting on April 26

The setback did not weaken the resolve of Ghetto fighters. Next day, a week after the outbreak of the revolt, new clashes erupted. The enemy could not yet conclude victory. On April 26, Stroop reported: "Without exception, all our units sent reports of meeting resistance. . . . It becomes ever more apparent that some of the most determined, rebellious Jews and outlaws have come to the fore." Rebel activity was particularly intense that day. Stroop lists 362 Jews fallen in the struggle. And The Fighting Organization was dealt yet another blow that day. Szymon Heller, the top rebel marksman, lost his life in battle in the shop district.

In the Ghetto the sea of fire raged ever more ferocious.

Last Letter of Mordekhai Anielewicz

On April 26, a letter from Anielewicz reached representatives of the fighting Ghetto on the Aryan side. This was the last known letter of the Uprising commander. It contains a report of the seven days' fighting:

> For the eighth day we are engaged in a life-and-death struggle. The Germans have suffered many losses, and during the first two days were forced to pull back. Then they brought in reinforcements in the

form of tanks, armored cars, artillery, and even planes. They instituted a full scale siege. . . .

The extent of our losses, i.e., of victims of execution and fire—men and women and children—has been enormous. Our last days draw near, but so long as we hold a weapon in hand we will fight and resist. . . .

Aware that our days are numbered we urge you: remember how we have been betrayed. The day of judgment for our innocently spilled blood will come. Send aid to those to be delivered at the last moment from enemy hands so they may keep up the struggle.

5

Heavy Battles of April 27; First Exodus from the Burning Ghetto: April 30

Skirmishes on Nowolipki, Nowolipie, and Leszno Streets, April 27: Their Tragic Conclusion

During April 27 bitter fighting raged on Nowolipki, Nowolipie, and Leszno. In houses at Nowolipki 39, 40, and 41 the inhabitants of fortified bunkers, maintaining steady contact with each other and possessing a fair amount of weapons, were preparing to offer resistance. Then, thanks to an informer, the Germans discovered the bunkers and opened fire on number 41. The Jews there refused to surrender and met a tragic end when their bunker was blown apart. Expecting the neighbors of these victims to be intimidated, the Germans ordered number 40 to surrender and forced their way inside. They were answered by a volley of shots, but they soon prevailed. Some of the captured took poison.

As the end approached, one of the fighters, thirty-six-year-old Helena Szterling, her ammunition gone, threw herself at the Germans and hit one of them in the face with her whip. She was killed on the spot. The other bunker fighters were either shot or sent to the *Umschlagplatz*.

Meanwhile, bunkers at Nowolipie 67 and 69 also fell. Their

defenders, including the laborers Szymon Szyntel and Henoch Hakman, perished in battle. A very tragic confrontation took place in the Jewish Fighting Organization bunker at Leszno 74. The Germans flooded the bunker with water, forcing the fighters to scamper from place to place, shooting all the while. Lost in the battle were the group's commander, Hersz Kawe, and fighters Zocha Bszezynska, Chana Brander, Tosia Cebulasz, Sara Kleinman, Aron Alter, Leyb Czerntakower, and Riva and Adek Rosenfeld.

Especially heroic was Lev Rudnicki, who, though losing blood, did not let go of his weapon until his last breath. Hersz Kawe, heavily wounded, made sure to give his gun and watch to comrades before he died. He bade them use the gun for fighting, and the watch to save and aid the living.

Young Halinka Rochman's Dedication

In the Leszno battle a deed was performed so extraordinary in courage and self-sacrifice that two surviving participants of the battle, S. Borg and M. Goldszteyn, cannot stop speaking of it to this day.

The youngest member of the combat group at Leszno 74 was Halinka Rochman. A young girl, she was the only daughter of a wealthy Hasidic family, but had grown up among revolutionary student circles; her firmness of character was revealed just before the insurrection. Halinka's father had obtained "good" papers and a secure place for the family on the Aryan side, but the girl refused to go. "I no longer belong to myself; my place is in the Ghetto with my comrades." With great pain she parted with her father and threw herself into the resistance movement.

For the April 27 fighting, Halinka Rochman was assigned to the group of Ruzha Rosenfeld, one of the most prominent warriors. In the midst of battle, Halinka suddenly noticed an enemy gun barrel pointed toward Rosenfeld. Without hesitation she shielded her commander with her own body and was felled by the bullet meant for the other. "My life is less important than Ruzha's," the dying Halinka said, "she's the commander; we need her more."

First Exodus Through Karmelicka Street

By April 27, both fighters and civilians holed up in bunkers were finding their situation unbearable; death lurked everywhere. Eyes were turning to the other side of the wall. That day a representative of the Polish underground appeared in the bunker at Karmelicka 5. His name was Tadek; he had arrived through the tunnel connecting the Aryan and Jewish sides of Karmelicka Street. Tadek brought bad news; it had become known through intelligence that the Germans planned to blow up the bunker the next day. He also brought better tidings; his comrades wanted to lead the bunker inmates to the Aryan side immediately. Bunker dwellers there were comprised of armed Farband and unaffiliated fighters—Symkha Korngold, a surviving eyewitness, was among the latter—plus civilians of both sexes and various ages.

The first exodus from the burning Ghetto began; it was far from the triumphant march out of Egypt. A few-score Jews crept through an underground tunnel and then a sewer, to arrive after twenty-four hours of groping in the maze, half dead, on the Aryan side in the area of the Old Ghetto at Grzybowski Square. From there they proceeded to a hiding place in a half-ruined house at Grzybowska 17. That house and neighboring ones at 11 and 13 of the same street became the goal and temporary refuge of other for-the-time-being survivors of the Farband.

Tragic End of the Niska Battle

Also on April 27, in the early morning hours, Stroop staged an attack on Niska Street where, from time to time, Jewish fighting groups used to appear. Stroop threw 320 troops into the attack, ordering them "to clean out the area on both sides of the street." The Jews resisted bitterly among the burning walls, shouting battle slogans the whole time, bringing Stroop to admit in his report that they "fired till the last moment." Even at the end when flames licked their feet the rebels still would not give up, and preferred to jump from windows and balconies, as they cried out against their tormentors. "With a curse on their lips, with outcries against Germany —the Fuhrer and the soldiers—they hurled themselves from burning balconies and windows," wrote Stroop.

As Niska was about to fall amidst screams of agony, rifle shots, and exploding bombs, the following scene unfolded. A young woman with an infant in her arms appeared on the balcony of a burning building. She stood still as the flames roared near her, and noticed Gen. Stroop in the street below. "I ask you no mercy," she shouted at him, "but remember, punishment will not escape you either!" When the flames were about to swallow her she clutched the baby and with a horrible shriek, jumped to the pavement. Her case was not isolated. Many a young mother covered the eyes of her child and jumped from a window or balcony into a crowd of Nazi murderers ready with their guns. Among those to perish on Niska was rebel activist Mariusz Lewit.

Major Battle at Muranowski Square: April 27

The heaviest fighting of the day took place on Muranowski Square in a confrontation that lasted from 10:00 A.M. until evening. Significantly, there Poles fought side by side with Jews. We have already mentioned that after the first two bloody battles of the insurrection, after some fighters had been taken prisoners and others escaped through a tunnel to the Aryan side, a Farband squad, led by David Apelboim, found itself stranded in ruins on Muranowska Street. Over several days Apelboim succeeded in gathering remnants of various shattered Farband groups from the brush factory area, Mila, and other streets—groups including those commanded by Pawel Rodi (Pinya Beshtimt), Kalman Mendelson, Janek Piko, Federbusz, Bynsztok, and Weinsztok. Apelboim also established contact with his Polish comrades within Maj. Iwanski's group. The two groups decided to undertake a joint action to fight their way through to the Aryan side of Muranowska Street, or at least reopen a tunnel and its exit at Muranowska 6 that had already been discovered by the Germans.

They worked out a precise plan whereby the Jews would take up three positions: one, in the partially destroyed house at Muranowska 7; two, in a neighboring house at Nalewki 38; and three, in a house across the way at the corner of Nalewki and Mila. Iwanski's men were to create a fourth station to get control of the tunnel entrance at Muranowska 7, and then move out onto Muranowski Square. A fifth position—unrelated to the above—was set up the morning of April 27 by an unknown Jewish group, probably affiliated with the Fighting Organization. It consisted of a wall of barrels placed at the point where Zamenhofa crossed Mila. From there too, the Germans would be fired upon.

This battle drew more rebel participants than any previous one. According to Stroop's report, fighters numbered 120 and were armed, at the least, with rifles, revolvers, 300 shells, and 100 grenades. Kalman Mendelson and Wladislaw Seidler, both of whom took part in the battle, later claimed that the group manning the position at the corner of Nalewki and Mila also possessed a machine gun, and that Iwanski's group was quite well armed and had automatic weapons. According to Stroop's report, his headquarters received an upsetting, anonymous letter from an informer in Iwanski's ranks about a joint Jewish–Polish fighting campaign about to take place on Muranowski Square. With the Germans thus forewarned, the chance of rebel success was much diminished.

Led by Police Lt. Diehl the Nazis marched into Muranowski Square through Nalewki and were immediately fired upon from all five rebel stations. This response was not sufficient to ward off a tank that Diehl then brought into action. Twenty-four Jewish fighters were killed, including Federbusz and Staniewicz; Kalman Mendelson and Pawel Rodi were among the wounded. Among Poles, Iwanski's brother, Waclaw, was killed, and his son was wounded. The insurgents were especially horrified by the serious wounding of their commander, David Apelboim. His fate has never been clarified, but we may assume that he perished in one of the later confrontations.

Despite the loss of the battle and the substantial number of casualties, the rebels were not totally defeated. At Muranowska, Iwanski's squad of ten was able to make an orderly retreat. Groups under Apelboim, Piko, and Pawel Rodi, in spite of their thinned-out ranks, were able to hold their positions. The Germans had still not weeded out all pockets of resistance in the area.

Jewish Fighters Break Through to the Aryan Side

That day, other fighting units around the burning Ghetto made an effort to reach the Aryan side. Ghetto chronicler, Emmanuel Ringelblum, the Polish underground press, and Ludwig Landau in his well-known account, report a series of such attempts. Ringelblum writes:

> At night the fighters broke through the walls with their weapons in hand, killing the Ukrainian guard or Lithuanian Shaulists, and then went into hiding on the Aryan side. More than once it was found necessary to combat Germans or even Polish police near the Ghetto. These pushes by the combat "Fives" through walls or underground passages took place at the square near Zelaznej Bramy, Krasinski Square, Teatralny Square, and Muranowski Square. At Teatralny Square, Polish police caught several fighters who had thrown a grenade and made off. Once seized they were shot in one of the bombed-out houses on Krolewska Street. (E. Ringelblum: *Polish–Jewish Relations During the Second World War,* ms. pp. 166–67.)

On Wednesday, April 28, at number 6 August Street, far from the Ghetto, a Gestapo agent detained a young man suspected of being a Jew. The captive broke free and fled. The agent fired. wounding him in the foot, but the fugitive returned the shot while jumping onto a passing streetcar. The man indeed was a Jew. Such incidents were not infrequent on the Aryan streets those days.

April 29: The Second Ghetto Exodus

A Polish underground report of April 29 gives us a terrifying picture of the condition of the still-struggling Jewish survivors in the almost destroyed, still-burning Ghetto. On that day, the Germans began full-scale demolition of the victims' last hiding places, the cellars and bunkers. Fully aware of their situation, especially of the constantly shrinking base of operations, active members of the Jewish Fighting Organization held a meeting on Wednesday night, April 28, in a Leszno Street bunker. They decided to make an all-out attempt to escape the Ghetto and join partisans; the task was given Regina Fuden ("Lilith") to round up scattered combat squads from the shop district and prepare them for departure. All were found except two groups, one of which was Hersz Kawe's. Kawe had been killed the previous day.

As they made ready to leave, the rebels had to suffer a most painful moment—parting from seriously wounded comrades who could not make the journey. Lea Korn, a fighter, stayed behind to protect these unfortunates who were told they would be brought later. The hope was ill-founded; within a few days the Germans discovered the bunker with the "infirmary" and murdered Lea Korn and the sick and wounded.

The rescue campaign of the Ghetto "exodus" had been arranged jointly by a representative of the Fighting Organization on the Aryan side and the People's Guard with the active cooperation of Franciszek Lenczycki, Polish labor movement veteran, and Wladislaw Gaik ("Krzaczek"), a lieutenant of the People's Guard.

On April 28 at 11:00 P.M., forty Jewish fighters who had just blown up a German warehouse at Leszno 72 entered the sewer. With weapons in hand, they passed through the canal and exited on the Aryan side at the corner of Ogrodowa and Zelazna. Led by Szalom Grajek ("Stefan") they temporarily established themselves in an attic at Ogrodowa 27, residence of their Polish protector, Richard Trifon, a laborer, anarchist, and revolutionary activist.

Friday, April 30, Gaik together with the Jewish courier Tuvia Szeingut transported the entire group in a truck to the woods in Lomianka, 7 kilometers from Warsaw. The expedition was carried out without complication before street crowds and frightened guards. At one point Gaik asked: "Men, are the grenades in good order?" Fortunately the grenades were not needed. The group stayed in Lomianka under the leadership of David Nowodworski and awaited the arrival of more combat squads from the Ghetto.

Regina Fuden's Act of Great Dedication

During the sewer crossing a deed was performed that ended in tragic heroism and surpassed all others in dedication. After completing the journey, Regina Fuden ("Lilith"), a young member of Hashomer Hatzair and daughter of a working-class family, declared her intention to return through the sewer to bring over remaining fighting groups. At first the leadership would not hear of it; the sewers had been flooded with water and passing through them meant almost certain death. Yet "Lilith" was ready for any sacrifice; she could not abandon her comrades.

Her superiors then consented to her expedition and gave her an escort, Szlomo Barczynski. The two, though tired and hungry after their first crossing, set out on the dangerous mission. They never returned. Aaron Karmi (Chmielnicki), a fighter, reports that "Lilith" was later seen in the Ghetto with a wounded foot, after a battle with the Germans in which she had taken part.

April 29: Skirmish at a Sewer Exit

The sewer and its exit were dumb witnesses to yet another tragedy that Thursday. After the first group had reached safety through the sewer, a second, under Benjamin Wald, decided to try the same. It made its way successfully to the exit, and, after growing impatient waiting a long time for a signal from outside to leave, ventured to depart on its own. Meanwhile, the Germans had found out about the first departure, and had stationed themselves around the exit. The utterly worn-out fighters now found themselves face to face with the enemy. After a brief, bitter, and tragic struggle, the band together with its leader perished in the unequal match.

April 30: More Fighting in the Ghetto

Twelve days had passed since the outbreak of the extraordinary Ghetto insurrection; by now even friendly observers on the Aryan side doubted whether the Ghetto warriors could maintain their resistance. For the April 30 entry in his secret chronicle, Ludwig Landau wrote: "The heroic battle, it seems, is reaching its end. Conflagration continues to rage and armed resistance grows weaker under pressure of the enemy's preponderant strength and the exhaustion."

Despite evidence to the contrary, that same April 30 Jewish fighting groups expanded the struggle to places in the Ghetto that had previously seen no action. On Przejazd Street a squad composed of remnants of sundry Farband groups set fire to a *Wehrmacht* arsenal. The squad was headed by Weinsztok (already known to us from the April 27 battle on Muranowski Square), Goldstein, and Lambert. The area resounded with heavy shooting.

Panic Among the Polish Police

Despite setbacks the revolt continued, causing ever-greater unrest among the enemy. With the number of its victims growing at the hands of vengeful Jews, the Polish police force was finally seized by panic. Official reports indicate that much of its force, unwilling to stick its neck out, refused or sought to avoid Ghetto duty. In general, the Polish police played a shameful role, both before and after, but especially during the Uprising. They hunted down Jews hiding on the Aryan side, extorted large sums of money from them, and, after leeching the victims dry, handed them over to the Gestapo. They robbed and tortured Jewish smugglers at the Ghetto gates. They belonged to the "evil spirits" that Ringelblum describes in his well-known book.

Like the police, large bands of Polish civilian extortionists, the so-called *shmaltzovniks,* also fed on Jewish misery. They lurked at Ghetto gates waiting for desperate refugees, then robbed, raped, and chased them back into the conflagration. They extorted from them, terrorized them, drove them from hiding places, and denounced them to the Gestapo. These activities became a livelihood and a sport for the participants, a band of outcasts including "golden" youth, hypocritical fanatics, and petty-bourgeoisie elements who wanted to inherit Jewish businesses and even professions. In this orchestra, money-grubbing Polish police played first violin. However, when the bullets and grenades of their victims began to rain down upon their heads, these same police showed their cowardice and kept away from dangerous Ghetto sites.

Proletarian and democratic sectors of the Polish underground combated both Polish police and the pathological, extortionist anti-Semites; they even carried out several assassinations against these elements. Yet the greatest influence in the underground came from the London-based rightist faction. Despite appeals by Premier Sikorski, little was done within the underground to combat extortion and other extreme anti-Semitic manifestations, such as collusion with the occupation forces.

6

Days of Crisis: May 1–10

May Day in the Burning Ghetto

Amidst fire and brimstone the insurgents decided to observe May Day, the annual workers' holiday, in a unique manner. The eve of the holiday, Friday night, April 30, several fighting groups attacked Nazi patrols at the Leszo 76–Nowolipie 69 sector, and both sides suffered losses. At 8:00 A.M. the following morning, fighters from the one remaining Fighting Organization bunker of the area, in the house at Leszno 74, tuned in radio Moscow, then arranged a seminar. The seventeen present stuck red flowers cut from linen into their lapels and Szakhne Feingold, veteran Communist activist, delivered a lecture. A participant in the seminar and survivor of the war, Bernard Borg, reports how no one present, no matter how aware of impending doom, doubted the words of the speaker: "Without question our struggle will have great historical meaning not only for the Jewish people but also for the resistance movement of all of Europe battling Hitlerism."

Borg continued: "Holding our weapons we softly sang the 'Internationale,' sensing the nearness of our final struggle, our own end." Similar sentiments were expressed by occupants of the central Fighting Organization bunker at Mila 18, even though they had no radio.

Before noon that day a combat group from Mila under Mordekhai Growas attacked a band of Germans from the rear near

Nalewki 43. Since the attackers wore German helmets, the enemy did not recognize them at first, and paid for the oversight with three lives. Nevertheless, they soon recovered and began shooting from all sides. The Jews, because of their superior knowledge of the terrain with all its pits and little holes, were able to return to their base unharmed. In the skirmish Itzhak Sukenik ("Losa") distinguished himself by not missing a shot.

At the same time several fighting groups, also on attack missions, left the bunker at Franciszkanska 30. These were composed mainly of the now battle-fatigued troops who had fought the early days of the Uprising in the brush factory area or on Nalewki Street. Then, on the evening of May 1, that bunker too celebrated the holiday, and once more the hushed strains of the "Internationale" resounded. The commander there, Marek Edelman writes in his memoirs:

> Never has the "Internationale" been sung under such extraordinarily tragic conditions, as an entire people goes under. The words and music and the singing reverberated among the charred ruins, bearing witness to a youth battling in the Ghetto who do not forget their meaning even in the face of death.

The sudden activation of the Jewish fighting groups in broad daylight alarmed the Nazi staff. Ordering an all-out attack against Ghetto ruins, Stroop hurled his mighty divisions amidst the roar of artillery against Jewish positions on Leszno Street.

That day the bunkers put up a more stubborn resistance than usual. Wrote Stroop on May 1, "No cases of voluntary surrender from bunkers were observed." Indeed a "wild" band of Jewish fighters set fire to an entire array of *Wehrmacht* possessions on Gesia and Nowolipie—stables, warehouses of hay, and similar items. Even at the *Umschlagplatz* itself the Nazis were given a come-uppance. Stroop reported: "In one instance a Jew, already being led to deportation, fired twice at a police lieutenant." That same day a squad of ten Jews tried their luck and escaped from the *Umschlagplatz.*

Stroop cites yet another piece of Jewish audacity. The Germans had begun to blow up sewer entrances to prevent their use as avenues of escape to the Aryan side. At one such mined entrance a Jewish fighter simply sneaked up under enemy eyes, snatched away the explosives, and made off.

Stroop ordered his night patrols in the Ghetto reinforced.

Three-day Battle at Franciszkanska 30

May Day also saw the beginning of the longest battle of the Uprising, that at the Franciszkanska 30 bunker. The struggle there lasted three days, from Saturday, May 1, through Monday, May 3.

The bunker had been built by the Ghetto supply office. A number of battle-scarred Fighting Organization groups were concentrated there, including those under Jurek Blones, Hersz Berlinski, Henoch Gutman, Jurek Grynszpan, and Marek Edelman. In addition to combatants, several hundred other Ghetto dwellers found refuge in the large bunker; they came mainly from the intelligentsia, and many were ill or near death. Among these was Samuel Winter, chronicler, communal activist, and supporter of the Jewish Fighting Organization. Tuvia Borzykowski reports that, despite trying conditions, the mood in the bunker was cheerful. There was much discussion, especially concerning the situation on the eastern front.

During the "cleanup" of Franciszkanska Street on the afternoon of May 1, the Germans stumbled onto the bunker and ordered the Jews to leave. When this order was ignored, the enemy began throwing grenades inside. The rebels maneuvered themselves out of the bunker into two positions behind the Germans, and caught them in crossfire. Dvora Baran, a fighter from Gutman's group, hurled the first grenade at them, chasing one and killing two.

A fierce battle followed. Reentry to the bunker became impossible—the Germans had blown up the main entrance. Fighting centered in the ruins of the house. The main objective of the defenders was keeping the invaders away from the second, well-disguised entrance. Finally, the Germans retreated with their dead and injured.

Two young fighters, Stasiek Briliantszteyn and Luszek Blones, distinguished themselves in the battle. But the rebels paid dearly for their temporary victory: Abraham Diament, one of their best marksmen, and young Abraham Eiger were killed. Eiger had enfortressed himself securely in an upper story of the charred house and from there fired upon the enemy. Even when completely surrounded, he still ignored the order to surrender. He fired his last shot then fell to the ground, his body riddled with bullets. Other fighters also perished, and their comrades buried them in a common grave that night after the Germans departed. Only Diament's body could not be found. During the fighting it had rolled down into the burning house and disappeared in the rubble.

The next day, Sunday, May 2, the Germans returned with reinforcements and initiated a campaign that lasted the whole day, with the rebels running from one position to another, leading their hunters into traps. The Germans were repelled, but not without great cost to the Jews. In the battle, group commanders Henoch Gutman and Jurek Grynszpan sustained serious wounds. Grynszpan was removed to a bunker on Zamenhofa, where he later expired.

Monday, May 3, the Germans appeared once more with fresh reinforcements, searching for the concealed bunker entrance. When they found it, they pumped in gas, sapping the dwindling strength of the rebels who were still struggling heroically. In his report, Stroop underscores this doggedness—insurgents shooting with pistols in each hand (their own and their dead comrades'), and the special gameness of women fighters.

In this final battle, half the bunker fighters fell, but not one was captured alive. The dead included Szanin Lent, Dvora Baran, Zipora Lerer, and Zisza Papier (from Berlinski's group). Some combatants and civilians succeeded in disappearing among the ruins to reach the rag pickers' bunker at Franciszkanska 22; others made their way to the bunker at Mila 18. The battle of May 1–3 was the last on Franciszkanska Street. By mid-May, the Ghetto segment of the street no longer existed; it simply had been razed.

Battle Around Stawki and Szczeszeliwa Streets: Streets: May 2–3

On May 2 there was fighting in other places too—in two factories on Stawki Street, at Transowia 36, and at the intersection of Wiszniewski and Serejsky. Jewish workers—many of whom perished as a result of their resistance—refused to give themselves up to the SS for deportation. On Szczeszeliwa Street, Jews took to shooting at the enemy from rooftops, as observed by Gen. Krueger, higher SS and police chief in Cracow, who had arrived that day in Warsaw. The same night, German patrols ran into heavy fire in the Ghetto. The next day, Monday, there were nineteen acts of armed resistance besides that at Franciszkanska 30.

In general, the Jews kept to the ruins by day but prevailed in the Ghetto at night. Stroop bears witness to this in a report of the night of Monday, May 3. According to his sentry details, armed bandits in tight groups marched openly over the Ghetto under cover of darkness.

Last Flicker of Resistance on Leszno: May 4–7

Stroop chose the next four days, Tuesday–Friday, May 4–7, to raze the shop district on Leszno, Smocza, Karmelicka, and neighboring streets. The Germans began the assault on May 4 at 11:00 A.M., with a renewed ultimatum to the Jews to surrender. No one responded. "Opening up the bunkers," Stroop was forced to admit in his May 4 report, "meets with ever-increased difficulty." Then, in a Dantesque scenario, the invaders chased the Jews to the rooftops by setting fire to buildings all around them. "A countless number of Jews," wrote Stroop, "perished in bunkers and flames."

May 5 was the same. Germans fired, burned, dynamited; Jews resisted actively and passively. "Today also," reported Stroop, "the Jews offered resistance in several places before being taken captive." The next day, Thursday, May 6, to Stroop's great consternation, the Jews appeared once more on Leszno Street with a fresh supply of energy and grenades. Actually, this was the Jews' last desperate military effort there, because the next day the end came, hastened by the Germans' increased use of gas.

The last Leszno defenders either fell captive or perished in battle. Only Ruzha Rosenfeld was able to shoot her way through the German line to disappear among the ruins. She, too, was never heard from again, and probably perished later in battle.

By Friday, May 7, with all of Smocza Street ablaze, only a few lone fighters remained to continue the struggle. The following incident is typical. From the corner of Smocza, a young Jew darted out of his hiding place and ran crouching toward some ruins. Two Germans armed with automatic rifles began chasing him. With amazing agility, he reached a house and bounded up the stairs, one floor after another. Stopping on a balcony to gaze wild-eyed at the scene below, the youth saw his pursuers aim their rifles at him. He then produced a grenade and hurled it at them, killing or badly wounding both, and quickly disappeared.

The above was related by Wladislaw Swietochowski, a Polish fireman at the scene, who had close affiliation with the Jewish and socialist undergrounds. His is the only documentation we have for that day on Smocza Street. Friday, May 7, that former habitat of Jewish poor and destitute breathed its last.

A Second Reconnaissance Squad Perishes

May 7 brought organized Jewish resistance yet another loss. After the earlier reconnaissance squad sent by Mila 18 met its doom, a second was dispatched with a similar mission—to set up contact with the outside to find ways of escape. The band started in the direction of the Ghetto wall and soon encountered an SS detachment. They traded fire, but the Jews proved no match for the enemy. All members of the mission perished, including Itzhak Sukenik, a superb marksman, and Lilke Simak, staff courier.

May 8: Death of Anielewicz and Co-Workers in the Mila 18 Bunker

The bunker at Mila 18 was built and originally occupied by a group of families of leftist-oriented smugglers and former back-pack porters, headed by one Srul-Iser. During the Uprising, several other leftist porter groups also moved in and, led by David Malowanczyk and Moishe Czompel—members of the Communist self-defense group before the war—they participated in the fighting on Muranowski Square. Malowanczyk was previously a *khesdl firer* (porter operating a pushcart) and Czompel [1] belonged to a well-known porter family. Among their group were men capable of splitting iron, who used to perform that and other feats of strength publicly.

Thanks to the intercession of the fighting groups of Malowanzanyk and Czompel, the proprietors of the bunker allowed the staff of the Jewish Fighting Organization, along with a substantial number of other combatants, to settle there. In that way, Mila 18 became central bunker of the Jewish Fighting Organization.

The bunker housed some three hundred persons, including eighty military personnel. The latter lived in very cramped fashion, but were most disciplined and orderly. They divided their own space into several subdivisions: "Ghetto," "Treblinka," "Trawniki," "Poniatow," and "Piaski"—symbolic revenge for the Ghetto and death camps. Gathered there were the stalwarts of resistance and other communal leadership: Anielewicz, his friend Mira Firer, his closest collaborators—Aryeh Wilner, Tosia Altman, Menahem Beigelman, Yehuda Wengrower, Rivka Pasmanik, and others. Ephraim Fondaminski ("Alexander"), Ghetto secretary of the Polish Workers Party and his friends; Michal Roisenfeld, Fighting Organization central staff member; Chaim Ankerman; Tosia and Franka Berman; Sarah Zszagel; Szyja Szpancer and Herman were also there.

Also sharing the bunker were group commanders Berel Broide,

[1] Diarist Chaim Frimer is mistaken in referring to these men as members of the underworld, an error resulting from confusing Czompel with Chumps.

Levi Grosalc, and Leyb Rotblat (of the "Akiva" group). The latter's troops included noteworthy women fighters like Perlman, Haldzband, and Neche Cukier. Here was Fondaminski's wife Liba (neé Zylbersztayn, code name "Ala"), Polish Workers Party and Fighting Organization activist. In brief, here were the mind and heart of the Uprising: the leaderships of the Jewish Fighting Organization, Hashomer Hatzair, and the Communists; plus activists and commanders in D'ror (a Zionist group), the Jewish Labor Bund, and Akiva. To this nerve center with its ongoing consultation sessions came couriers, and from it went the missives and bulletins that reached to the other side of the wall.

From the accounts of Chaim Frimer, who lived there till the fatal May 8, and Tsivia Lubetkin, fighter and D'ror activist, we can picture the general mood inside the bunker. The atmosphere was comradely and cheerful, with much discussion and singing. Songs taken most seriously were "Es brent," "Mir kumen on," and the Hebrew, "Sfineinu ha-nodedeth"; Yiddish folk and Soviet songs completed the repertoire.

From the beginning, the German high command had taken great pains to discover the whereabouts of the central bunker, together with the insurrection leadership. Stroop's reports claim over and over the imminent discovery of the hideout with the "insurrection's top leadership," or "P.P.R. Central." Only on May 7 is there a statement mentioning knowledge of the bunker's location with the "narrow party leadership" and "Z.Z.W." (the Farband—apparently Stroop was not clear in his terms). Stroop also assures his superiors: "Tomorrow the bunker will be opened by force."

Saturday, May 8, the Germans were indeed able to trace down the bunker—their source of intelligence is still unknown—and they surrounded the area, occupying all five entrances. The entire civilian population surrendered and came out, but the fighters remained inside to ward off the invaders. Convinced, after blowing up the entranceways with grenades, that the rebels would not give up, the Germans then injected gas. The victims began choking; someone suggested that everyone commit suicide. Leyb Rotblat then gave poison to his mother, Miriam (Marie), prominent educator and directress of a children's home, and to her adopted daughter, and then shot himself. Dorka Goldszteyn, an indirect witness, said that before death the rebels all sang their various anthems. It is clear that almost all fighters there perished, including Anielewicz, Frimer, Fondaminski, and Wilner. Tsivia Lubetkin believes that Anielewicz committed suicide, but Chaim Frimer claims that he succumbed to the gas after soaking his head in a bowl of water in an attempt to revive himself.

Few survived—those who were closer to the exit only fainted from the gas. Among the latter were Michal Roisenfeld, Liba Fondaminski, Tosia Altman, Beigelman, and Wengrower—who were later rescued by Lubetkin, Frimer, Israel Kanal, and others, and taken unconscious to the Aryan side by a People's Guard expedition. The dead comrades who remained in Mila 18 could not be identified because the bunker was subsequently blown up. Nor is it known how Malowanczyk, Czompel, and their comrades met death. There are indications that they perished later in battle.

The tragic end of the top leadership of the resistance came as the heaviest blow to the surviving fighters; the Nazis, too, appreciated its significance. Arriving at the site of the demolished bunker, Stroop commented regretfully: "The persons I would be most desirous of interrogating are now dead."

Thus fell Mordekhai Anielewicz, "one of the finest and noblest warriors, who from the beginning, put his life at the service of his people," according to Emmanuel Ringelblum, who knew him well from their joint underground work. Thus fell Aryeh Wilner, heroic liaison officer of the Jewish Fighting Organization, who in March of that year, 1943, gritted his teeth rather than betray his comrades during torture-interrogation at Gestapo headquarters. And Ephraim Fondaminski, passionate Jew, fiery revolutionary, who had declined the offer of his Polish professors to save him, in order to share the fate of his people and the Fighting Organization. And Levi Grozalc, product of Jewish secular schools; Leyb Rotblat, who joined the Jewish milieu from assimilated environs; fiery-worded Sarah Zszagel; and all the other fighting men and women from their respective circles and movements. One idea united them: to combat Hitlerism for a free world where proud, jubilant Jews could exist.

The Third Ghetto Exodus

The story of the People's Guard expedition that attempted to save the fighters of Mila 18 is taken from "The Sewer," an account written by fighting group leader Hersz Berlinski in 1944 while he was in hiding on the Aryan side. He died later that year in the fighting for the liberation of Warsaw.

On April 29, Simkha Rathayzer ("Kazik"), a participant in brush factory battles, made his way out of the Ghetto to the Aryan side. Once there, with the aid of Jewish representatives and the People's Guard, he organized a third mission to the Ghetto with the goal of bringing over, among others, the Mila 18 group, including Anielewicz. Rathayzer brought two Polish sewer workers to the Ghetto with him, Czeslaw Wojciechowski and Waclaw Sledriewski, recruited for the project by Wladislaw Gaik of the People's Guard.

For Mila 18, they arrived too late—it no longer existed. At first, they also missed Lubetkin, Frimer, and Kanal who had returned to the bunker to rescue their unconscious comrades. With heavy heart, Rathayzer and his fellows began crawling toward Franciszkanska 22, where a group of local fighters was stationed.

The Jews and Poles from the Aryan side who had set up the rescue expedition included the following—Jews: Itzhak Cukierman, Jurek Zolotow, Ryszek Mozelman, Zalman Frydryk, Tuvia Szeingut, Rathayzer, and Shlomo Szlakman, a former Yiddish actor from Bialystok who disguised himself as a railroad worker with the name Stefan Koluszko, and adopted the pseudonym "Kolejarz" as well. The Poles were all from the People's Guard, with the exception of the sewer workers already mentioned: Jozef Malecki ("Senk"), plenipotentiary of the general staff; political activists Franciszek Lenczycki and Wladislaw Legec, along with the latter's wife, Stanislawa; plus Lt. Gaik, officer in charge of the project.

In the bunker at Franciszkanska 22 were fifty armed fighters. Having received the crushing news of the destruction of the Mila 18 staff on Saturday, the leadership at Franciszkanska dispatched a group of scouts headed by Aaron Briskin ("Pawel"). They were to pass through the sewer on Tlomackie 5 to obtain relief on the Aryan side, but instead fell into an enemy trap on that street and perished somewhere. We shall see that that group at least managed to return German fire and break through to Miodowa Street. Next evening, Sunday, a second reconnaissance squad left Franciszkanska 22 and also disappeared. Only a third such party survived to return with news of the arrival of Rathayzer's expedition in the Ghetto.

For the trip back to the Aryan side, fifty fighters dragged themselves through putrid waters, their weapons bound to their necks and backs, many bent under the weight of unconscious comrades saved from Mila 18. Each minute of the trip felt like an hour in hell, and each hour a day. Yet, even under such horrid conditions, humor was not entirely absent. Chaim Frimer tells the following episode. Among the fighters creeping through the sewer was a simple Jew named Baruch, who turned out to be a *shlemazel,* a misfit, and so the butt of teasing from his companions. "Remember," one of them said, "it's all over with you if you continue to creep that way—I'll kill you myself."

"Good, it's better you kill me and end my troubles," Baruch answered.

"I'm ready to carry out your wish, but first you have to pay me 100 zlotys for your bullet."

Baruch began to bargain in earnest—he could only pay 50 zlotys: "I can't afford any more," he pleaded. Everyone burst into laughter, the only heard in those gruesome hours.

Approaching the Aryan sewer exit on Prosta Street at 8:00 A.M., May 10, the worn-out wanderers heard what sounded like a great explosion. Indeed it was: People's Guardists outside had terrorized the Polish police on patrol and blown off the manhole cover—in full view of an astonished throng of Poles. They also had a truck waiting, and the driver, Stanislaw Tarczynski, of Warsaw, sped them off to Lomianki Forest within half an hour. There the group was joined by Marek Edelman and other comrades already there (this journey was described earlier). The joy of the liberated rebels was marred, however, by the death of Yehuda Wengrower, who had been carried unconscious from Mila 18. He was buried in the forest.

Second Tragic Battle at the Sewer Exit

Not all fifty fighters who made their way through the sewer reached the light of day. With Gaik hastily loading the truck in anticipation of the appearance of German police, only thirty-four persons climbed aboard; fifteen more were to await its return down below. Meanwhile the police, SS men, and Latvian Fascists arrived and surrounded the opening, having laid mines there. Those inside, knowing nothing of this and losing patience over their long wait, emerged, to find themselves face to face with the enemy. As under similar circumstances ten days earlier, a tragically unequal confrontation ensued, pitting the strong and well-armed against a heap of human skeletons; all fifteen ghetto fighters were murdered by Nazi grenades. The dead included the commanders Hochberg and Blones, fighters Szlamek Szuster, L. Romanowicz, and Pnina Sandman.

Heroic Deaths of Jurek Zolotow and Ryszek Mozelman, Couriers

That a second fighting group was able to make its way to a partisan camp did not mean that Fighting Organization couriers despaired of further struggle within the Ghetto. May 10, the same day as the sewer incident, couriers Jurek Zolotow and Ryszek Mozelman were to receive a package of weapons for the Ghetto. On their way to the assigned meeting place at Bankowy Square, however, they were spotted by Polish police. Zolotow threw a grenade at them, but had no chance against the bullets raining down on him. He was killed on the spot. His companion, seriously wounded and bleeding profusely, was then dragged by German soldiers to nearby Zabia Street, close to Saski Park, and shot.

Thus ended the first twenty-two days of insurrection. The turning point of this first phase of Ghetto struggle came May 8–10, with the death of the central command and the exodus of the second fighting group. Now came the second and final stage.

7

Battles Among the Ghetto Ruins: May 10–Mid-July

Last Phase of the Uprising

Monday, May 10, the Ghetto struggle entered its final phase: sporadic skirmishes among ruins of a gutted Ghetto. Offensive or defensive actions could not be coordinated even to a slight degree by the end of April and early May, and the combat squads of this phase, named for the ruins, were called *khurves grupn*. These latter groups, operating in the rubble of the Ghetto-turned-wasteland, were comprised of surviving remnants of both the Fighting Organization and the Farband under mostly "veteran" commanders. Commanders from the Fighting Organization were Zekhariah Artszteyn, Joseph Farber, Bloiszteyn, and Szymon Melon, one of the new leaders. From the Farband, Chaim Lopato, Janek Piko, and Pawel Rodi.

New fighting groups also sprang up, especially from the bunkers, and were often led by spontaneously chosen commanders. One of these was Berek, a Jewish member of the Polish Socialist Party, and a former apartment-house watchman in the Ghetto. Earlier he had participated in freeing Polish underground officers from Pawiak Prison. Some other new commanders were Laizer Szerszen, a Treblinka escapee; Moshe Koifman, metalworker; and the porter, "Moishe Bolshevik" (pseudonym).

The Ghetto dwellers were living then both above and beneath

the ruins. Especially in the "wild" and brushmakers' areas there were still several thousands in undiscovered bunkers, and thousands more just wandering in the ruins. Never remaining in one spot, the wanderers were no sooner discovered than they vanished among the skeletons of former buildings. They roved in packs through the rubble in search of food, water, and clothing.

After May 10, the bunker base of the remaining fighters changed catastrophically. Here is an eyewitness report from an architect, engineer, and bunker builder named Goldman on the condition of the *khurves* people.

> Human specters pop out of cellars, faces unshaven, clothes tattered, weapons in hand. . . . After passing through several cellars and attics we find ourselves in some kind of house on Muranowska. It is night; people come into the courtyard and huddle in a shed. On the floor lay bricks with pots atop them. Dirty matted-haired women cook something. The children, resembling little forest creatures, demand their portions. We are warmly received and offered food and drink.

Despite the squalor, an atmosphere of cordiality and mutual aid was found among ruins dwellers. There was also brutality. Goldman tells of struggles over weapons and of someone being disarmed.

> While on our way, a wild episode was enacted by the blue light of burning sulphur in a courtyard on Franciszkanska Street. Someone carrying "illegal" weapons was being disarmed. A minute later someone else was called out of the cellar and told to give up his weapons. The bearer refused. Then a crack in the face with a rifle butt and the bearer fell down, his weapon snatched from his hand and ammunition bag from under his belt.

A steady "market" or "bazaar" operated among the ruins. At night, when the Germans left the Ghetto, people would emerge from their bunkers and lairs to deal in cigarettes, matches, and candles produced from the inevitable plunder of abandoned hiding places and burned-out buildings.

Among the sea of ruins the human specters, armed with weapons procured or found, continued their stubborn resistance. Monday night, May 10, several *khurves* groups attacked German patrols, prompting Stroop in his May 11 report to bemoan the lack of gas to inject into rebel bunkers. The Jews took cheer at this scarcity and repeated the previous night's attack. Stroop claims that 53 Ghetto "bandits" perished that day in battle and 133 the next during further bloodshed.

Germans Panic and Flee Once More

Wednesday, May 12, a group of fighters from bunkers on Swientojerska and Walowa, checking the Ghetto for possible avenues of escape, suddenly found itself face to face with a large German patrol. At first the fighters were terrified—until they discovered that the Germans were equally moved at the sight of a wild-looking bunch of Jews emerging from the dead stillness of the ruins, apparently sprouted from the very ground on which they stood. Recovering their composure before the enemy, the Jews began shooting, causing the Germans to take to their heels and leave a dead soldier behind. From the corpse, the Jews took ammunition and a map of the Ghetto.

Intensified Grenade Battle: May 13

May 13,[1] twenty-five days from the onset of insurrection—after the Ghetto had been destroyed by fire, after the enemy had used poison gas, not quite a week after the destruction of the Fighting Organization command, Stroop still found it necessary to write of intensely renewed though flickering fighting in the Ghetto.

> While liquidating a certain bunker a full-scale armed confrontation ensued, during which the Jews not only fired from .08 calibre revolvers and from Polish *Wis,* but also showered SS men with grenades. When part of the bunker crew was forced to come out and was

---

[1] Ber Mark gives this date as Saturday, though the day was actually Thursday—*trans.*

about to be searched, one of the women, as often happened before, pulled a grenade from her bloomers and with lightning speed threw it among the soldiers. In an instant she was back in her hiding place.

The remaining members of the bunker crew, who refused under any circumstances to give up, met death when the Germans blew up the bunker. Stroop admits that Germans also perished in the action.

An eyewitness, Joseph Lehman, tells of a bitter fight that same day at a bunker at 3–5 Bonifraterska Street. The Germans had sniffed out the hideout and laid siege to it, but the Jews inside were determined not to come out. Sarah Rosenboim, a fighter, crawled to the entrance and hurled a grenade at the Nazis, wounding several. The latters' comrades then bombarded the bunker with grenades, but during the chaos that had erupted those inside had sneaked away through rear alleys to temporary refuge on Franciszkanska. The occurrence of this skirmish is confirmed by a Polish police report that mentions a confrontation on Bonifraterska in which two Germans were badly wounded.

Also on May 13, a battle took place at the bakers' bunker in the courtyard of a large house at Walowa 6–Swientojerska 30. Aryeh (Leon) Naiberg, a fighter and eyewitness, describes the truculent resistance of this bunker group. Naiberg says that during the fight the Germans seized a Jew named Biloier and questioned him about the whereabouts of his fellow Jews. In reply, Biloier, an elderly man, smacked the interrogating SS officer in the face and cried out: "Murderer! Here are the Jews!" He was immediately shot. This incident is given credence in Stroop's May 13 report: "Getting information from captured Jews about locations of bunkers known to them has lately become an impossible task."

Soviet Air Raid the Night of May 13

The night of May 13, the Soviets launched a major air raid amidst explosions, huge conflagrations, and renewed fighting in the Ghetto. The air attack came in response to an SOS from the underground Polish Workers Party leadership in Warsaw to Georgy

Dimitrov in Moscow, who in turn passed on the request to the Soviet Committee for National Defense. The routing of this bulletin, through the partisan base in eastern Poland, carried the approval of the local partisan commander, "Janowski" (Leon Kosman). The wire requested an act of retribution for liquidation of the Ghetto, in the form of bombing German military installations in Warsaw.

Indeed, the flames of the burning Ghetto served as an excellent guide for Soviet planes. The attack lasted two hours, from 11:30 P.M. to 1:30 A.M., with bombs hitting many objectives, such as SS barracks, but also several Polish sections and the Ghetto vicinity. Many were killed and wounded. A number of Jewish groups tried to exploit the raid to attack befuddled German guards and escape from their trap. Stroop mentions a number of losses in his ranks in the next day's report.

There were at least three such escape efforts. One on Okopowa Street was totally unsuccessful, but others on Mylna and Bonifraterska showed partial positive results. Dr. Poliszuk, a Jew, tells of these attempts in a report he later turned over to the underground Jewish National Committee.

> During the May 13 air raid over Warsaw, four of us, ready for anything, went out amid the din of falling bombs and anti-aircraft artillery. We made our way through Mylna Street. On May 17, we met a contingent of armed Poles in the recesses of the street. The night of May 18, we escaped to the Aryan side.[2]

In the commotion of that night the well-known fighter Pinya Beshtimt (Pawel Rodi) along with the fighting porter, "Krzywonos," and five members of their group apparently made their way out of the Ghetto, using their contacts in Wolia, a Polish workers' district. Once on the Aryan side, Rodi distinguished himself as an important underground activist, largely engaged in transporting weapons to the last Jewish positions in the country. He died in battle during the Polish Uprising in August 1944.

---

[2] Dr. Poliszuk was later betrayed by Polish hooligans and killed.

Rooftop Battles: May 14

The next morning, with many Aryan streets in Warsaw showing evidence of the previous night's air raid, more fighting broke out in the Ghetto. By this time Jews were concentrating their attack ever closer to the Ghetto borders, in order to maximize opportunities for escape. On May 14, a group of fourteen fighters worked its way to a rooftop not far from the Ghetto border, and from there fired for a long time at the Germans. Yet another Nazi bigwig was granted the chance to observe an amazing battle: *Waffen SS* Maj. Gen. von Herf, head of personnel in the *Reichssicherheitshauptamt* in Berlin. That night more shooting and clashes ensued among Ghetto ruins. The Polish police report for May 15 states: "By day, powerful explosions blast the ear; at night, shots crackle near Ghetto borders. Shooting comes from hand weapons and both light and heavy machine guns."

Demolition of the Great Tlomackie Synagogue: May 16

After four weeks of incessant fighting, the battered, bleeding Ghetto had not yet capitulated. Stroop well-understood that the battles—though not of the magnitude of earlier ones—were not over, but decided to give official notice of their termination. On May 16 he informed his superiors: "The former Jewish quarter in Warsaw no longer exists." Actually, this was a political ploy: Stroop did not write "the Ghetto no longer exists."

In honor of "the great historical victory," and as symbol of the demise of Warsaw Jewry, Himmler ordered Stroop to destroy the Grand Synagogue at Tlomackie 5. That magnificent building had been erected in 1877 in German Neo-Renaissance style, according to the design of Leonardo Marconi, a famous Italian architect. A *Wehrmacht* sapper team under Stroop's supervision placed a huge charge of dynamite under the building; the noise of the explosion shook all of Warsaw. At his trial in Warsaw, July 1951, Stroop defended his action with the claim that a Jewish fighting group had been hiding in the building. That may have been true—we know that on May 8 and 9 two reconnaissance groups escaped from Franciszkanska 22 and headed toward Tlomackie, where they were attacked by Germans.

Stroop's *Grossaktzion* (grand action—his term for suppressing the Uprising) was officially completed on May 16, at 8:15 P.M. Since he was aware of various fighting groups still entrenched in the Ghetto ruins, he dispatched the 23rd Police Battalion under Maj. Otto Bundke, with an order to "comb through" the last ruins of the Ghetto and liquidate remaining Jews. Just at that moment, however, new fighting groups appeared, as if sprung from the ground. An eyewitness who crept out of his bunker that day for a brief moment describes the scene:

> Suddenly we noticed some male figures in the street. They were coming from Zamenhofa. Instinctively, we jumped to the side and hid behind the wall of the building. They stopped not far from us. I saw they were wearing helmets and high boots; I didn't notice any rifles. At first we thought they were a German patrol, but hearing them talk we realized they were our own. We approached them. They were dressed in German uniforms; under their belts were hidden revolvers and grenades. They were young and tall. From Mila Street, they believed fighting in the Ghetto was finished but sought revenge, and wanted to fight until the end; at night they ambushed German patrols. We parted with a handshake. That was May 16, 1943.

Ghetto Fighting Until the End of May

The next morning, May 17, the Polish police record noted the following: "The Jewish squads virtually crawl out of the ground unexpectedly to attack Germans." Because of this, it stresses, SS divisions had to be reinforced. Even so, Stroop's liquidation order of the previous day stayed on paper; police battalions left in the Ghetto could not cope. "Despite the six weeks' long assault with a wide variety of weaponry," wrote the leftist underground periodical "Glos Warszawy" in the May 28 issue, "despite the razing of the whole Ghetto area by fire and the use of gas, the handful of defenders has never been subdued. At certain points the fighting even flares anew."

The police and SS did everything to make life among the ruins impossible. They cut off the flow of water and poisoned that which was left, poured kerosene on food supplies, and tore up sidewalks and pavement. Still sporadic outbursts of Jewish fighting went unchecked.

May 18 marked a substantial exchange of fire among the ruins. On May 19, skirmishes broke out on the corner of Gesia and Nalewki, where groups under Szymon Melon were active, and at other points on Mila Street. Germans used machine guns and Jews hurled grenades. Two German policemen fell, and the Jews thus obtained more weapons.

At Mila 44, a local bunker group put up a desperate struggle after being betrayed by a Jewish informer. The latter paid with his life, snuffed out by a fighter's bullet. The Germans injected their lethal gas and soon total silence reigned over Mila, once home of the Jewish poor and proletariat. The former seat of resistance command lay in its death throes.

May 20, the fighting moved to Nowolipki and Nowolipie streets. The Polish underground press of May 22 wrote: "The struggle in the Nowolipie region has broken out once more." Also, "The Jewish resistance movement is still present in the ruins of Nowolipie, and the shooting of heavy machine guns can yet be heard."

Polish police reports of May 20–24 contain frequent mention of continued fighting: "On the side of the German police and SS who are engaged in making the Ghetto secure there are bloody sacrifices, and the number of dead German functionaries is too large."

Last Battle of the Farband: Gryzbowska Street

While Ghetto fighting continued, some Fighting Organization and Farband groups were also to be found, in relative safety, on the Aryan side. These groups remained in constant contact with the resistance inside the Ghetto, and even participated in battles. A band of Farland survivors with ten members armed with grenades and revolvers, headed by Pawel Frenkl, occupied a bunker at

Grzybowska 11. On May 11, it was discovered by the Germans, who besieged it and ordered the Jews to surrender. The members refused, and Germans trying to break in were met with bullets. The latter, as usual, barraged the structure with grenades, killing most of the fighters immediately, including Frenkl. Three of those captured were executed later.

The Tragic End of a Jewish Fighting Organization Group in Praga: May 25

In the Warsaw suburb of Praga, a celluloid factory at number 11 November Street became the hideout and meeting place for a ravaged band of Fighting Organization members. There the survivors of Mila 18 were nursed from the brink of death, and there couriers and emissaries to partisan groups in the Lomianki Forest came to receive and deliver their messages.

According to a May 25 Polish police report, a fire broke out in the factory and spread rapidly because of the celluloid; soon the whole place was ablaze. Later the police found the charred bodies of Tosia Altman and two other Jewish fighters, all three of whom had come from Mila 18.

A fourth fighter in the factory, Eliezer Geller, managed to escape with burns and wounds. The fifth, Meir Szwarcz, a courier, fled from the burning building to the house of a neighbor, a Polish woman. She hid him in a closet from the police who came searching for him. They did not find him, but when the kind woman opened the closet door she found a corpse. Szwarcz had suffered a heart attack and died without a groan.

Deaths of Other Ghetto Warriors

Enemy bullets and grenades, intelligence operations of Polish Fascists, or chance claimed many more members of the Fighting Organization and unaffiliated fighters who had been saved from the burning Ghetto by Polish anti-fascists. In the cellar of the house at

Ogrodowa 19, already known to us, belonging to the "good spirit" Richard Trifon, a way station had been set up for Ghetto fighters en route to partisans. The "good spirit" protected, as the "evil spirit," the ingrained anti-Semite, destroyed. But German police forced their way into the cellar and, after a short desperate effort at self-defense, the Jews were slaughtered to the last man.

The *shmaltzovniks* and sundry informers were the greatest blight upon Jewish combatants and civilians who had fled the Ghetto. Wolf Rozoswki, a Fighting Organization squad commander (also a member of Tsukunft), became one of the victims of those beasts that preyed upon Jewish misfortune. Rozoswki had gone to a way station at Zurawia 24, apartment 4, belonging to Polish Socialist underground activist, Eugenia Wonsowicz-Leszczynska (wife of Jewish Labor Bund activist Samsonowicz), whose apartment quartered a Fighting Organization propaganda setup and arsenal and was the base for many illegal activities. Rozowski did not tarry there long; he went into the city still unable to rid himself of *shmaltzovniks* and informers and was finally killed by the Gestapo.

On July 7, a bloody drama unfolded in the house at Washington 80, where Stefan Pokropek, a Polish Socialist, lived. Pokropek was involved in important tasks for the Jewish fighters, chiefly weapons procurement. His home was a hidden meeting place for the Jewish Fighting Organization, as well as headquarters for its courier, the heroic Tuvia Szeingut ("Tadek") of Hashomer Hatzair. July 7, the Gestapo suddenly forced its way into the apartment. Both Pokropek and Szeingut offered resistance but were soon overpowered and murdered.

To close the file on many rebel fighters on the Aryan side, we take a big leap to the beginning of 1944. In a Fighting Organization bunker at Prozna 14 lived the fighters Jacob Feigenblat ("Jacek") of Gordonia; Sigmund Igla, of the Jewish Labor Bund, and Guta Kawenoki, all of whom maintained contact with the underground. At the beginning of 1944, their bunker was betrayed and the three perished after a brief defense.

Not all Ghetto fighters now on the Aryan side suffered that fate. An entire group headed by Itzhak Cukierman ("Antek") survived under trying conditions to participate in the Polish Uprising in

August 1944. Its members included Tuvia Borzykowski, Hersz Berlinski, Tsivia Lubetkin, Marek Edelman, Pola Elster, Joseph Erlich, and I. Celemenski, a courier. Berlinski, Elster, and Erlich fell during the Uprising.

Also on the Aryan side, a group of Jewish communal activists kept in touch with the above group of fighters. Among this group were Dr. Leon Feiner, Salo Fiszgrund, and other central Jewish Labor Bund figures; Dr. Abraham (Adolph) Berman and other Jewish National Committee members; Menashe ("Nastek") Motiwiecki, a People's Guard officer and Jewish activist who also died in the August 1944 Uprising; and Janina Bir, Communist activist. This group had taken a number of difficult tasks itself: organizing relief for the Jews living like hunted beasts on the Aryan side; purchasing arms for those remaining in the last ghettoes and camps in Poland; and last, maintaining contact with Jewish bodies abroad, to arouse public opinion toward providing relief and taking other appropriate actions.

Feiner, chairman of the outlawed Bund Central Committee, Berman, of the secret Jewish National Committee, plus their close associates, distinguished themselves in their work. Through various means Feiner succeeded in sending reports and alarms abroad—as did underground activists Cukierman, Gotesman, and others.

Pawel Finder, first secretary of the Central Committee of the P.P.R., sent reports of Ghetto fighting and SOS appeals to internationally famous labor movement leader Georgy Dimitrov in Moscow. Both Feiner's reports and Finder's secret dispatches are now available in archives; they are important documents of the era of Ghetto battles.

Aaron Briskin's Group Battles at Miodowa 41: May 27

Today in bright daylight heavy shooting broke out on Miodowa Street. Several Polish and German policemen were killed, also some of the attackers, one of whom turned out to be a Jew. It is believed the skirmish was between a German and a Jewish group because yesterday lively shooting had been heard among the ruins, and it was said that certain detachments had broken through to the other side.

The well-informed Polish democratic underground daily, "Nowy Dzien" of May 27, also gives information about that confrontation:

> A fighting group attacked and shot two officers of the Polish police on Miodowa Street opposite the district courthouse. After carrying out the mission the group retreated from the scene. Polish police and gendarmes then arrived, and the fighters shot at them with revolvers and threw grenades. The skirmish began at 10:00 A.M.

The noted underground activists Mr. and Mrs. Legec, whose task was to take into their home on Szczygia Street Jewish fighters escaping from the Ghetto, were convinced that the aforementioned fighting group was Briskin's. Briskin was among those who had left the Franciszkanska 22 bunker for Tlomackie Street to find a route to the Aryan side. Before settling into Miodowa 14, the group wandered much and had many confrontations with Polish police. From Miodowa they made contact through the Legecs with the People's Guard. In the end they were betrayed by the house watchman who summoned police and perished in an unequal battle. The informer, too, met his death—sentenced and executed by the People's Guard. Briskin, the heroic warrior of Miodowa 14, was a member of the Communist youth.

Last Battles on Nalewki

At the end of May, the last bunkers fell—betrayed by Jewish informers who in turn were later punished by Jewish fighters—and the last battles among the ruins on Nalewki, the main avenue of the Ghetto, were fought. Here, too, the remaining Fighting Organization groups under Zekhariah Artszteyn, Itzhak Bloiszteyn, and Joseph Farber allegedly operated. The last fighting groups on Wolynska Street also perished at this time.

But the month ended with an especially bold attack by a straggling band of Jewish fighters against an SS detachment conducting what had come to be a daily convoy of captured civilian Jews to be shot among the ruins. In broad daylight, the SS squad was cut to ribbons and the condemned got a new lease on life. This incident provoked the Nazis to reintroduce armored cars into the Ghetto. In his June 1 report, the police recorder acknowledged: "Conditions in the Ghetto have deteriorated."

On May 31, Gov. Gen. Frank called a meeting in Cracow to discuss security in the country, and Gen. Krueger in his report as security "minister" noted that he had "received word from security police in Warsaw that the Jews continue to carry out attacks and murders." In other words, fighting in the Ghetto had not yet ceased.

Krueger states further that suppressing the Uprising and liquidating the Ghetto are the most difficult police tasks, but, by command of the *Fuehrer,* they must be carried out. Krueger acknowledges the Jewish rebels' courage, especially that of the women who, he claims, distinguished themselves by their strength and militancy.

Last Battle of Commander Zekhariah Artszteyn: June 3

One of the best Fighting Organization commanders, still heard from at the beginning of June was Zekhariah Artszteyn, a member of D'ror. With his squad he had moved from Nalewki to Bonifraterska to be closer to the Ghetto border. Several eyewitnesses independently report that his group was attacked on June 3, not far from a demolished house on Bonifraterska 13. Artszteyn's strategy was to try a diversionary action, then attack from the rear. When the Germans opened heavy fire, some of the Jews stationed themselves in the burned-out house and replied with scattered shooting. The Germans then moved closer to the house, concentrating their entire force upon it. At that moment, Artszteyn and the rest of his fellows let themselves down from the eaves and attacked the invaders from behind. Being caught between two fires would, under normal conditions, have put an end to the Germans. But the young Jewish fighters were so tired and emaciated from hunger that they lacked the strength to conduct a substantial grenade assault—their throws fell short of the mark. Five warriors, including a girl, were lost, while the Germans lost three of their force. Surviving Jews escaped among the ruins, but a few days later, Artszteyn tried once more to break out of the Ghetto and that time perished.

Reports of Fighting in June

On Sunday, June 5, Janek Piko, last Farband commander, died. Piko (a pseudonym, his real name remains unknown) was a simple man belonging to the common folk, who managed to attract to his fighting unit many former "roughnecks" whom he then transformed into dedicated fighters.

On June 8, the Polish underground publication "Glos Warszawy" wrote:

> Although a number of journals have reported the demise of fighting in the Ghetto, a handful of fighters still functions there. In the past few days they have carried out a number of forays over the walls, killed several gendarmes, and forced [the enemy] to enlarge its forces.

That Ghetto fighters still functioned is further confirmed by a June 15 Land Army intelligence report stating that day and night the Germans sent small detachments of Ukrainian and Latvian auxiliary SS into the Ghetto with machine guns and grenades where they pried everywhere and demolished bunkers. In just one bunker on Leszno they discovered a well-concealed band of 150—that same Leszno where no trace of a Jew even existed. The Land Army report concludes: "One may surmise that in Ghetto territory there is still a large number of armed Jews ready to defend themselves."

Further confirmation of continued fighting in the Ghetto in June comes from a letter written by a native German woman visiting Warsaw to a top police bureau in Germany. This woman, whose name is unknown to us, complains about poor living conditions and other inconveniences to which German civilians in Warsaw are subject "due to the attacks of Jews and gangs." She blames Nazi police in Warsaw for allowing the allegedly top secret liquidation plan to be divulged to the Jews. "That action was to have lasted no more than three to four days," she writes, "but it has been dragged out five weeks with no end in sight."

Our last piece of information comes from a German Warsaw police document recommending a citation be awarded Capt. Ederer of the *Schutzpolizei* for success in combating "Jewish–Bolshevik bands" in the former Jewish quarter, in June 1943.

The value of the three preceding documents lies in confirming that such fighting actually took place; none, however, gives the precise sites of June battles. We have been able to obtain this missing information from Aryeh Naiberg and Dr. Richard Levi (Walewski), who participated in, and later recalled, some of the fighting during that month. Through them we know there were clashes on Bonifraterska, Muranowska, Berish Majzels, Swientojerska, and Walowa streets. They even listed names of some fighters, like Janka Gontarska, Klonski, Moskowicz (an engineer), and the porter, "Moishe Bolshevik."

The Uprising Dies Down in July

The aforementioned German document mentioning Capt. Ederer refers to fighting in the Ghetto not only in June, but also as late as July! Ederer was praised there for battling a group of nine armed "Jewish bandits" in the former Ghetto in July 1943. Leon Naiberg and Moishe Flamenboim, a metal worker, tell of July fighting on Swientojerska, Walowa, Franciszkanska, Muranowski Square, and Zamenhofa. On Walowa 4, they say, Szymon Melon's fighting group hailed bullets upon Nazis marching into the Ghetto singing the venomously Jew-baiting "Horst Wessel Song." After first taking to their heels, the killers soon returned and forced the Jews to flee toward Franciszkanska Street.

On July 2, blood flowed from a well-disguised, heroically defended porters' bunker at Franciszkanska 37 where, at great sacrifice, the Germans were repelled. Among other fighters, the young son of a porter perished. Over his son's body, the grief-stricken father swore revenge upon the enemy.

In another incident dated July 7, a *khurves grup* passing by Nalewki 23–25 was attacked by Germans and fired back. In spite of such continuing acts of resistance, the Uprising gradually flickered out. The food supply, and human strength, was dwindling. As the Germans again took to blowing up ruins, drinking water also became unobtainable. Aryeh Naiberg tells that "At night we wandered over the courtyards, like lunatics, in search of water."

One goal remained: to flee the valley of death. Whoever was able, escaped, but by now the sewer routes had been rendered useless—the Germans had filled them with water and blown up the exits. The only way out was to sneak at night through enemy patrols—for this many paid with their lives. The last groups to leave safely and with weapons in hand did so on September 23 and 26. Among them were our two witnesses, Naiberg and Levi. They left behind a huge wasteland shrouded in silence.

The Ghetto's Last Cave Dwellers and Their Final Battle

The eerie stillness was pierced from time to time by the cracking of bullets—not all survivors had managed to leave the Ghetto. Until the end of 1943, at least, there remained sporadic groups of armed Jews that possessed revolvers and grenades. Prisoners in the newly erected SS concentration camp on Gesia who were used to clear away the Ghetto rubble would see armed young Jews keeping at a distance from prisoners in order to fire at the SS. As a result, the SS stood in mortal fear of going too deep into the Ghetto area. The Jewish fighting groups, driven by animal hunger, also came out of their lairs to pass beyond the bounds of the Ghetto wilderness in search of food. At such times they often traded fire with the SS. The last Jews perished either by SS bullets or from starvation.

The very last source of information we have of a fighting group among Ghetto ruins is the July 7, 1944 issue, No. 27, of the Polish underground publication "Informacia Wschodnia i Narodowa"

(Eastern and National News). It tells of an attack on a German police battalion passing through the Ghetto in mid-June 1944! For three of their men killed there, the Germans raided the Ghetto and executed the twenty-five Jews they captured. This took place after the Uprising had been crushed by every means available to the Nazis.

In underground caverns of the Ghetto, individual Jews survived till the very end, until the outbreak of the Polish Uprising in August 1944. David Bialograd, a barber, witness to the last phase of the Holocaust, lived to declare the liberation.

II

Documents of the Uprising

COMMON ABBREVIATIONS AND SYMBOLS
USED IN THE DOCUMENTS

Ar.	Archive
Min.	Ministry
C.Ar.	Central Archive
I.M.	Interior Ministry
A.K. (Polish)	Land Army
J.H.I.	Jewish Historical Institute of Warsaw (headed by the author)
J.N.C.	Jewish National Committee
K.K.	Coordinating Commission
. . .	Deletion found in original document
[. . .]	Author's deletion
[ ]	Author's insertion
( )	Used in original document

The document section has been somewhat abridged from the final Yiddish edition of *Uprising. —trans.*

1. WARSAW GHETTO, MAY 15, 1942

First Appeal of the Anti-Fascist Bloc

To the Jewish Masses!

We stand at the doorway of great events and of enormous, decisive battles. Throughout the winter the Red Army has engaged in substantial attacks, forcing the fascist enemy to retreat from a whole series of occupied territories. It has delivered him mighty blows, upsetting the enemy's plans and forcing him to commit all his forces to the front—forces that would have otherwise been used for Hitler's promised spring offensive. Huge, well-equipped, well-prepared detachments of troops and the powerful reserves of Soviet Russia stand ready for further attack. Without stop, Soviet industry concentrates all its resources on the struggle in preparation for victory. On the heels of the German Army a movement of partisans has arisen, bringing dissension and sabotage.

Hitler has been forced to admit that only by incredible physical and moral strain has the German Army avoided breakdown. The SS machine pressures and terrorizes the German soldier into bleeding at the front. At the same time, food rations for the German civilian population already wearied by steady air attacks have been cut again. Instead of bread the people are fed on promises of an always remote rapid victory.

Because of defeats at the front and a sense of insecurity in occupied territories, the fascist beasts have further tightened the noose around the necks of enslaved peoples. A dreadful campaign of physical extermination is being conducted against anti-fascist warriors and patriots in Norway, France, Belgium, Holland, and Yugoslavia.

The brutal fascist invader is trying to root out the liberation movement in Poland—mass expulsion of Poles from the Pomeranian and Posen regions, annihilation of Polish peasants, systematic man-hunts throughout the cities, mass executions in Warsaw, and deportation of thousands of victims to Auschwitz—links in an endless chain of the invader's violation of Poland.

The beastly extermination campaign against the Jewish population is also heightened. Hitler sees as his historic mission the ultimate annihilation of Europe's Jews and he carries out his plans at an increasingly rapid tempo. Rivers of blood flow from tortured Jewish masses. Vilna, Slonim, Baranovitch, Khelm, Lemberg, Lublin, and tens of other cities and towns mark the bloody path of Hitler's murderous bands.

Merciless slaughter of thousands of harmless Jews; mass executions of thousands of Jewish settlements; poisoning by gas of the aged and young; shooting of women, hospital patients, children in orphanages—these are the noble deeds of Nazi hangmen rushing to please their leader, as though it would be sinful to tarry. . . . Tens of thousands of Jews, confined behind Ghetto walls, die of starvation or are cut down by typhoid and consumption. At the same time the Nazi executioners speed up their work: shoot down, murder tens of thousands of Jews, wipe entire Jewish settlements off the earth.

Jewish masses dare not possibly succumb to despair or confusion. With all their might they must exert themselves to join the anti-fascist fight of oppressed peoples. Like others, they must take to bloody battle with the enemy, especially to conduct destruction and sabotage in his rear flanks. In the anti-fascist struggle of the persecuted peoples, the Jewish masses must assume a proper role.

This struggle requires unity and closing of ranks. Awareness of the need for unified struggle has already taken root in broad strata of the Jewish masses. There are those, however, who still wait around for miracles. They do not realize that the only path to freedom and deliverance is struggle. They still do not understand that the times require joining forces to fight the damned invader, that the demand of the hour is to set up a national freedom front.

Jewish people! Jewish workers! Jewish youth! Gather your forces and pool them for battle! Stand united shoulder to shoulder in a common front against fascism.

Only destruction of the Nazi war machine by anti-fascist armies together with the masses of oppressed peoples will finally put an end to our enslavement and lead to full social and national redemption of the Jewish masses!

All resources of the Jewish people must now be united to the one and only goal: the struggle for freedom and redemption, and ultimate victory against the fascist enemy!

J.H.I. Ar.
Ring I. "The Call," [1] no. 1, May 15, 1942

2. WARSAW GHETTO, JULY 3, 1942

Jewish Resistance Action Prior to the First Liquidation

Friday, July 3, a notice was posted in the Warsaw Ghetto concerning the execution of 110 Jews (10 policemen and 100 civilians) for disobedience to the regime.

The alleged reason cited was a fight that broke out at the eastern railway station between Jewish workers, headed by Robak, a student, and a Polish machinist who then called the Polish police. Shooting broke out; the Jews resisted; Robak died in the skirmish.

C.Ar. of I.M.
Delegation[1] Ar. File 458
Bulletin from Information Dept. concerning situation
   in Warsaw Ghetto.
Trans. from Polish

---

[1] "The Call" was the organ of the Anti-Fascist Bloc. Three issues were printed, one of which is extant. The editorial board consisted of Joseph Lewartowski (P.P.R. [Polish Workers Party, Communists]), Shakhne Zagan (Left Labor Zionist), and representatives of Right Labor Zionist and Hechalutz.

---

[1] The London-based Polish government-in-exile—*trans.*

3. WARSAW GHETTO, LATE JUNE 1942

Community Conference in Zczitos—Nowolipki 25

Present: Zagan, Orzech, Blum, Joseph Lewartowski (P.P.R.), Ringelblum, Giterman, Alex, Landau, Kirszenboim, Szyper, Zysza Frydman, and others.

Agenda: Conditions in Warsaw Ghetto. . . .

Statements by Frydman and Szyper made a strong impression.

Zysza Frydman [1] advocates faith as a solution to Jewish problems: "I believe in God and in a miracle, God will not let His people Israel be wiped out. We have to wait for a miracle. War against the Germans is senseless! The Germans can put an end to us within a few days as in Lublin. If matters continue like this any length of time a miracle will occur. You, my friends, who count on the Allies, why do you despair?—you believe they will win; then they will bring you freedom. . . . The comrades who lean toward the Revolution and the Soviet Union, you believe capitalism is done with, that only the Red Army will liberate you. All right, believe in your Red Army. . . . Dear friends, persevere and have faith and we will have freedom!"

Szyper [2] does not advocate self defense; defense means destruction of the entire Warsaw Ghetto: "I believe we'll succeed in saving the core of the Warsaw Ghetto. It's wartime; every people brings sacrifices. We too must do the same in order to preserve the nucleus of the people. If I could be convinced that we couldn't succeed in preserving the core of the people, I'd come up with other conclusions. . . ."

The conference broke up with the resolution to meet again.

---

[1] An Agudath Israel activist from Lublin.

[2] Dr. Itzhak Szyper, well-known historian and leader among the General Zionists.

The developments that followed have made any further conferences impossible.

Hersz Berlinski: *Memoirs*
Ar. of J.N.C.

4. BIALYSTOK, APRIL 1943

Tenenboim's [1] *Report on the Community Conference in Warsaw Ghetto in April 1942*

In April 1942 after long negotiations among various parties a conference took place in Warsaw among party representatives and a number of trusted personalities from Jewish self-help circles. Representing the movement—Itzhak,[2] Joseph Kaplan (Hashomer Hatzair), and the author of these words. From the Bund—Maurycy Orzech and Lucian Blit.[3] From the party [4]—Sak (Left Labor Zionist), Emmanuel Ringelblum, and Zagan. From the Zionists—Bloc, Dr. Szyper, and Kirszenboim. From the Communists—Finkelstein.[5]

We presented precise information on the destruction of Lithuania and White Russia. We established that this storm wave is rapidly approaching the province. We insisted upon mobilization of all resistance resources, and stepping up the fight against the enemy. If we have no chance to meet the enemy in the field—through partisan warfare, diversionary tactics, and sabotage—let us at least

[1] Mordekhai Tenenboim (changed to Tamarov on a forged passport), active in the underground resistance movement in the Warsaw Ghetto, was sent as representative of the Jewish National Committee in November 1942 to Bialystok Ghetto to help organize armed resistance there. Together with Daniel Moskowicz, a Communist, he served as commander of the Bialystok Ghetto uprising in August 1943, and perished in that battle. While with the Ghetto underground in Bialystok he kept a diary which also included memoirs of the Warsaw Ghetto. The form of the diary was a letter to comrades in the Histadrut in Palestine. He also described the tragic conferences of the communal activists in the Warsaw Ghetto, but confused a conference described elsewhere by Berlinski, which took place in March, with that discussed by Berlinski in Document 3 and Nowotko in Document 5, and held in late July.

[2] Cukierman.
[3] Blit is incorrect; should read Abrasza Blum.
[4] Right Labor Zionist.
[5] Pseudonym for Joseph Lewartowski.

defend ourselves at home. We believe that this is the only path for the heads of the Jewish community to take at this time. True, it is difficult to function with this outlook on life, but one must acknowledge the truth—one dedicates oneself to this task, or in practical terms, nothing will happen.

Kirszenboim: "Correct, in Lithuania events were evaluated accurately. It's possible the same will happen in other places, but we can be sure that in Warsaw, the heart of Europe, the Germans will not indulge themselves. In the Warsaw Ghetto, with over four hundred thousand Jews, annihilation on this scale is unthinkable. We, the collective of the Ghetto may not play with fire. Let us not bring misfortune with our own hands; there's nothing the Germans can't find out about."

Orzech began with an evaluation of the political and military situation: "The war (April 1942) is entering a decisive phase. A second front will be opened up. When Germany will be occupied in the last stage of the war, oppressed peoples will be called upon to rebel. Meanwhile we have no choice; we should not be chauvinists —not only Jews suffer and perish. Thousands of Poles are also led to their deaths. In the current situation our sole task is psychological self-defense. If a Jewish policeman is ordered to hang a Jew he should not do it. Objectively, there is no basis for a procedure predetermined to fail. Jewish masses will be summoned in directives by the Polish working class to a common struggle. The tactic suggested here has no workability without broad revolutionary aid from the Polish public. Conclusion: Jews should go into hiding."

Zagan came up with a mouthful of revolutionary rhetoric. Only Finkelstein sided with us. Of the others, Giterman[6] went furthest—he always sided with the "youth."

Since then, deportation was begun in Lublin, the second largest Ghetto, and the first such in the province there. The optimists can no longer argue that what has happened is merely revenge on Jews in the Soviet Union; they now feel the approaching storm.

We looked for contacts and support outside the Ghetto. We met

---

[6] Itzhak Giterman, director of Joint Distribution Committee and Democrat cultural activist.

with the P.P.R. (Polska Partia Robotnicza), i.e., the Communist Party, reorganized under the slogan of "people's unity in the freedom struggle." The latter was ready to cooperate with anyone on a program of immediate and direct battle against the invader. We needed such a contact.

Why did we hook up with the Communists?

In the official branch of the Polish movement, under Sikorski's wing, the main tasks were seen as propaganda, education, and civil struggle—especially economic. In any deed that involved direct confrontation with the occupation forces, they saw provocation. "The time has not arrived yet. We have to save our strength and reserves until the day will come that the Polish Government will issue the command to take up arms. Because of the repressions that would follow each deed of active resistance, there is as yet no basis for acts of resistance. The chances are not even; therefore we have to wait."

But we could not wait. Each day liquidation grew more and more likely. Each day was a continual race against Himmler; therefore we sought out a different partner and discovered one in the P.P.R.

[. . .] in the Ghetto, utmost unity of action, conference upon conference and communal tasks. A sort of "popular front" was formed: Communists, D'ror, Hashomer Hatzair, the Party,[7] and Left Labor Zionist. The "Bund," affiliated with P.P.S. and through that with Sikorski's crowd, was forced to adhere to "the time has not come" line.

> J.H.I. Ar., Underground Ar. of Bialystok Ghetto, to
> comrades in Palestine, Bialystok, 1943
> *Trans. from Hebrew*

---

[7] Right Labor Zionist.

5. WARSAW, OCTOBER 22, 1942

Dispatch from Nowotko [1] to Dimitrov [2]
re Conference of Jewish Communal
Representatives of Warsaw Ghetto,
Late July 1942

Here are more replies to your questions. Through the initiative of our party in the Warsaw Ghetto a united front of all Jewish parties [3] has been set up, with the exception of the Bund, which sharply opposed us and was especially virulent against the Soviet Union. In July [1942] the Germans began liquidating ghettoes everywhere. Jews not working in war industries like shoemakers, tailors, etc. are taken out and gassed. That is how the Germans did away with all the ghettoes around Warsaw. In Warsaw itself, out of four hundred thousand Jews hardly fifty thousand remained; all others were led away.

At the beginning of the liquidation of the Warsaw Ghetto our representative [4] at a meeting we initiated of delegates from various parties, made several proposals: resisting mass murder, organizing large detachments for self-defense and using these groups to break loose from the Ghetto and join partisan divisions.

The proposals were not accepted because intensification of liquidation would result.[5] Instead the Bund proposal was accepted: apply for aid to the Polish government-in-exile, England, and America. Soon everything fell through: no resistance against mass

[1] Marceli Nowotko, First Secretary, Central Committee, P.P.R.; murdered by the enemy.

[2] Georgy Dimitrov, hero of the Leipzig Trial, Secretary General of the Comintern.

[3] Anti-Fascist Bloc.

[4] Joseph Lewartowski.

[5] Approving the proposal were Left Labor Zionist, Hashomer Hatzair, Hechalutz, and the Bund (according to memoirs of Dr. A. Berman).

murders was offered. Only a segment of our comrades got out of the Ghetto to join partisan ranks.

Nowotko

Ar. of Inst. for Party Hist.
Polish Comintern Files
Trans. from Russian

6. WARSAW GHETTO, MID-AUGUST 1942

Secret Conference on Recruiting Partisans in the Ghetto

In the first half of August, a conference was held in O.B.W.[1] Present were Pola,[2] Lewartowski, and Kaplan.[3] The conference resolved to send delegates who have Aryan features and are fluent in Polish to the partisans. The partisan leadership wants male candidates. No precise details on training, lodging, or transportation are available. The conference also resolved to train partisan cadres.

Hersz Berlinski: *Memoirs*
Ar. of J.N.C.

[1] *Ostdeutschebauwerke*—a German firm in the Warsaw Ghetto on Gesia Street. Thanks to its Jewish director, Alexander Landau, resistance sympathizer, several Jewish anti-fascist activists were able to hide out there, including Lewartowski and Kaplan.

[2] Pola Elster, Left Labor Zionist activist, participant in founding of the underground National Council of Peoples Poland

[3] Joseph Kaplan, activist in Hashomer Hatzair and Anti-Fascist Bloc.

7. WARSAW, AUGUST 31, 1943

SOS from Berezowski [1] to Zylberboim [2] re Reasons for Lack of Mass Uprising During First Ghetto Liquidation

[...] here and there incidents of active resistance took place. Houses were barricaded [...] Such expressions of resistance, of course, ended with immediate total liquidation. These cases were only sporadic, there has been no active rebellion on a large scale. The reasons: (1) illusory hopes aroused by the enemy; (2) self-interest of members of the *Judenrat* and other officials able to save themselves; (3) the problem raised by the policy of collective responsibility;[3] (4) realization that help will not come from over the [Ghetto] walls; (5) absence of any response from abroad.

The enlightened segment of the Jewish working class and of the intelligentsia came to fuller understanding of the need for active resistance. This in spite of the unfeasibility of a larger-scale rebellion due to the atmosphere and conditions the Germans had deliberately created in and around the Ghetto.

This notion was rejected by conservative Jewish elements, claiming there would be immediate retribution by the German leadership. Their alternative was catastrophic obedience for the entire area.

C.Ar. of I.M.
Docket 458, pp. 71–76.
Trans. from Polish

[1] Dr. Leon Feiner, chairman of the underground Central Committee of the Bund in Poland, member Council for Relief to Jews. Died immediately after the liberation. The SOS was sent through the intercession of Polish socialists.

[2] Samuel Zygelboim (Artur), Bund representative on the National Council of the Polish government-in-exile in London. Committed suicide in May 1943, in protest against the world's feeble reaction to Nazi mass murder of Polish Jewry.

[3] Refers to Nazi policy of holding all Jews responsible for the act of one—*trans.*

8. LONDON, SEPTEMBER 23, 1942

Gen. Sikorski's Cable to Gen. Rowecki in Poland re Position of Government Toward the Jews [1]

In connection with cables 3262 and 3242 I assert the following: In its policy vis-à-vis the Jews, the Government ascribes totally to the principles of democracy, in the name of which the Allied states conduct the war. The Government completely supports these principles. We must remember that the position of the Anglo-Saxon world concerning anti-Semitism is unequivocal. The best means of assuring full support for our interests is by our showing and granting equal rights.

> C.Ar. of I.M.
> A.K. Ar.
> Bulletins to Kalina, No. 354
> *Trans. from Polish*

9. LONDON, OCTOBER 19, 1942

Gen. Sikorski's Cable to Poland re the Need to Combat Anti-Semitism

The Polish Government has protested repressive decrees against Polish Jewry; our foreign legations treat Jews just like other Polish citizens. Lavalle's government has been unanimously condemned by the entire French society for capitulation and servility to the Germans. Anti-Jewish acts have no support there even among rightist politicians; Catholic circles categorically oppose anti-Semitism; I

---

[1] This document is important in showing how, under pressure from international democratic public opinion, Gen. Sikorski was forced to demand better treatment of Jews from his followers.

therefore plead with you that in Poland the principles of democracy come broadly to the fore. We must remember that the war is carried on precisely for these ideals.

Sikorski

C.Ar. of I.M.
A.K. Ar. Cable 4349
Trans. from Polish

10. WARSAW, OCTOBER 18, 1942

Report on Combat Preparations of the Farband

A.[1] established contact with the Ghetto where there apparently are 150 utterly dedicated, well-armed Jewish fighters. He conducts business negotiations with that group, allegedly providing large amounts of arms in return for cash or articles of clothing. Ketling says he has been to the Ghetto and observed extensive self-defense preparations, such as disguised cellars, underground passages, and a tunnel several meters long. In the bunkers and tunnel there are large quantities of food and weapons. The tunnel has an exit on the Aryan side. Through Ketling, the aforementioned Jewish group seeks a contact with Theodor,[2] in order to coordinate major sabotage actions they plan to carry out shortly.

Man

Ar. of Inst. for Party Hist.
Documents of Special Military Court
File 46
Trans. from Polish

---

[1] Arpad—Capt. Cesary Ketling, leader of a Polish Democratic battle detachment. In October 1942, Pawel Frenkl and other Farband military leaders made contact with him.

[2] Polk. Niepokulczycki—leader of a Land Army diversionary detachment.

11. WARSAW GHETTO, OCTOBER 30, 1942

Notification by the Jewish Fighting Organization of Carrying Out of a Death Sentence against a Traitor, Jacob Lejkin

We hereby inform the public of charges lodged against the officers and functionaries of the Jewish *Ordnungsdienst* in Warsaw, already mentioned in the notice of August 17. A death sentence against Jacob Lejkin has been issued and executed. Lejkin was a representative of the *Ordnungsdienst* leadership. The sentence was carried out October 29, 6:10 A.M.

Future acts of reprisal also will be carried out with utter severity. At the same time we wish to inform that the following have been placed under charges:

1. The Warsaw *Judenrat* and its presidium;
2. The shop foremen and administration, for exploiting and persecuting the workers;
3. The group leaders and functionaries of the *Werkschutz* for torturing the workers and the "illegal" Jewish population.

Reprisal will be applied most severely.

> J.H.I. Ar.
> Ringelblum Ar. II.
> *Trans. from Polish*

12. WARSAW, DECEMBER 10, 1942

Notification to London re Danger of Liquidating the Warsaw Ghetto

H.K. and Stem.[1]
According to the information stemming from the city administration, a full-scale liquidation of the Warsaw Ghetto is anticipated in January, 1943.

Kalina

C.Ar. of I.M.
Bulletin 1080
Trans. from Polish

13. WARSAW, DECEMBER 12, 1942

Memorandum to London re Self-Defense in Warsaw Ghetto

In Warsaw Ghetto, street executions and random shootings of passersby have begun again. Small shops are also being liquidated. The so-called Toebbens shops have been completely cut off from the rest of the Ghetto. Among the surviving Jewish population desperate self-defense projects have sprung up.

Kalina

C.Ar. of I.M.
A.K. Ar. Bulletin 171
Trans. from Polish

---

[1] Cryptonym of Polish government-in-exile in London.

14. WARSAW, DECEMBER 3, 1942

Waclaw's [1] *Memorandum Containing Demands of the Fighting Organization for Weapons*

On December 2, 1942, I contacted the emissary of the Bund, Mikolaj,[2] and the representative of the Jewish National Committee (J.N.C.), Jurek.[3] During the meeting Jurek gave me the enclosed copy of bylaws of the Coordinating Commission (K.K.) and of the Fighting Organization, which represent the Jewish community of Warsaw. The charter was passed by the K.K. in the Ghetto the night of December 1, 1942. All doubts expressed by Mikolaj concerning the right of the J.N.C. to represent the Jews before the Polish authorities have been cleared up. From now on both delegates, Mikolaj and Jurek, jointly represent the K.K. in agreement with the authorization provided by the charter.

Concerning organizational efforts among Jews in the province at large, the initiative is to be taken by J.N.C.

Both K.K. delegates, Jurek and Mikolaj, stressed the need for immediately supplying the Jewish Fighting Organization with arms, because they have no doubt that extermination action in Warsaw can recommence at any moment. (Recently such [a campaign] was carried out on a large scale in the streets and shops.) The liquidation of a number of shops, and lately, the total segregation of Toebbens' shops from the Ghetto proper indicates that basically the extermination campaign proceeds uninterrupted.

Intensification of the campaign is expected due to the appearance of a large number of beggars. (Shop work does not pay more than subsistence: 10–20 deco of bread and soup. Those who have no

[1] Waclaw, pseudonym of Henryk Wolynski, head of Department of Jewish Affairs for the A.K. High Command.

[2] Dr. Leon Feiner.

[3] Pseudonym of Aryeh Wilner of Hashomer Hatzair.

articles to sell "steal" a few hours away from the shops in order to beg.)

Given this situation Mikolaj and Jurek request the following:

1. A larger number of weapons; the present ten pieces do not suffice to organize armed rebellion or any campaign other than of an individual nature.

2. Providing for and organizing arms purchase. They are checking into possibilities of raising their own funds for this purpose. (My opinion: from the standpoint of control the purchase should be conducted by us.)

3. Instruction and instructors. The Jewish fighting element was schooled to a degree through pre-war Polish military service. There is a shortage of qualified instructors because such persons carry out police functions, and so are not trusted by the Fighting Organization.

Concerning point one, I want a multiple increase in weapons provision, to reach approximately twenty pieces.

I request a quick decision.

Waclaw

File 456, p. 84.
Trans. from Polish

15. WARSAW GHETTO, DECEMBER 2, 1942

Charter of the Jewish Fighting Organization

In order to organize the Jewish population of the Warsaw Ghetto against the annihilation campaign of the occupation, and in order to protect the Jewish population of Warsaw against traitors and agents who cooperate with the Nazis, a coordinating commission has been set up comprised of the [Jewish Labor] Bund and Jewish National Committee. The latter, in turn, is composed of the following parties:

Zionist Organization, Right Labor Zionist, Left Labor Zionist, Revisionist Party, Hechalutz, Hashomer Hatzair, and D'ror.[1]

The functioning of the Coordinating Commission is based upon the following bylaws:

COORDINATING COMMISSION

1. By virtue of the agreement concluded between the Jewish National Committee and the Bund, a Coordinating Commission has been established for Warsaw.

2. The goal of the Coordinating Commission is:

    a. Organizing defense of the Ghetto in case of further deportations.

    b. Protecting the Jewish masses in the Ghetto against the paid agents and occupation lackeys.

    c. Calling into existence a combat organization, setting its direction, and controlling it.

3. Each party is entitled to one delegate to the Coordinating Commission.[2]

THE FIGHTING ORGANIZATION
STRUCTURE

1. The primary unit of the "sixth," headed by a commander.

2. These "sixths" are organized by shop. Heading a shop is a command, comprised of a commander and two deputies.

3. Heading the organization is a command of five persons,[3] including the commander-in-chief.

4. The "sixth" is formed according to party affiliation. Where

---

[1] P.P.R. belonged to the Jewish Fighting Organization and had a representative in its high command, Michal Roisenfeld. In the official bylaws submitted to the Polish government-in-exile and Land Army command, P.P.R. is not mentioned for fear the former bodies, rabid anti-Communists, would break off contact with the Jewish emissaries.

[2] P.P.R. representative on the Coordinating Commission was Alexander (pseudonym of Ephraim Fondaminski), secretary of the P.P.R. organization in the Ghetto (after Shmul Meretik and Ziga Gotlib were killed).

[3] They were Anielewicz, Berlinski, Edelman, Roisenfeld, and Cukierman.

that is not possible, a mixed group is to be set up. In the course of the campaign the unaffiliated will also be drawn into the cells.

5. In choosing the leadership only the qualifications of the candidates are to be considered.

ARMAMENTS

1. Arms include: hot weapons, axes, knives, brass knuckles, and scalding and incendiary materials.

2. Each cell member is to be armed.

3. Each area is to be provided with weapons and other means of carrying out military action.

OVERALL POLICY OF THE MILITARY CAMPAIGN

1. In case of a further deportation action resistance will be carried on under the slogan "We Will Not Give Up One Jew."

2. A terrorist campaign will be initiated against the Jewish police, Jewish communal leaders, and the *Werkschutz.*

3. To protect Jewish masses active combat will be conducted against shop administrators and foremen, the open and secret Gestapo agents.

IMMEDIATE TASKS

1. Setting up the cells and the leadership.
2. Arming the cells and the shops.
3. Fund raising.
4. Preparation by shop commands of:
   a. Precise plans of the areas (warehouses, cash boxes, *Werkschutz,* management deployment).
   b. List of dangerous elements.
   c. Precise plan of action in each shop territory.
5. The preparation by the high command of an overall campaign plan for sabotage and terrorism.
6. Propaganda to arouse the community to resistance and struggle.

TITLES

1. The combat organization assumes the title: Jewish Fighting Organization.
2. In order to maintain tight contact between both authorities, the Fighting Organization and the Coordinating Commission, the commander of the former will sit in on the meetings of the latter.

Representing the Coordinating Commission vis-à-vis the military forces will be the delegate of the Jewish National Committee, code name Jurek; and of the Bund, pseudonym Mikolaj.

C.Ar. of I.M.
Delegation Ar. File 458, pp. 81–82.
Trans. from Polish

16. WARSAW GHETTO, DECEMBER 4, 1942

Appeal by the Jewish Fighting Organization

Uncertainty about the morrow poisons every minute of the bitter enslavement of the Jewish community of Warsaw. Each day brings forth various "reliable" information, intrigues, rumors, and deadlines concerning the fate of the Warsaw Ghetto. We are "given" two weeks, three weeks, three months, or four months to live. Nerves, already on edge, quiver. Courage, already drained, causes us to waver between hope and resignation.

Have we learned nothing from this horrible experience? Shall we allow ourselves to be lulled by a good word from one or another German murderer spread by Jewish stool pigeons, venal traitors, or gullible persons?

There is no doubt that Nazism has set itself the task of annihilating the Jews and carries it out in stages to fool the Jewish masses. It cuts deeply into the throats of its victims and . . . throws the next victim a bone before the slaughter.

Let us therefore open our eyes and boldly face the truth.

We put no trust in any "stabilization campaign." [1]

We remember all the lies, beginning with "resettlement" in the east, and ending with numbers, mass distribution of identification cards, selections, and registrations.

We all know the truth about the gigantic slaughterhouses in Treblinka where hundreds of thousands of fathers and mothers, brothers and sisters have been exterminated so inhumanely and with beastly refinement.

We do not accept for one minute the "new" demands about forming Jewish ghettoes—this is a trap where any moment the door between life and death can be slammed shut.[2]

The *"Umschlag"* has been eliminated; amnesty for the "illegitimate" Jews; "jobs" and "food" for all Jews—what a cynical joke. The murderer toys a bit with the defenseless victim before letting the bloody ax fall on his head.

Jews, residents of the Warsaw Ghetto, watch out; don't believe one word or trust one deed of the SS bandits; death lurks. Remember the latest "campaign"—snatching "labor" details for Lublin. They needed "tailors" and grabbed up old people and children. They needed people for "labor" and just took persons as they were: bare and naked. The story repeats itself—greetings and letters arrive from persons sent to Lublin. We are reminded of the "letters," the "reliable" greetings manufactured by the Germans from Brest, Minsk, and Bialystok. We are reminded that in Lublin there is a Belzec where tens of thousands of Jews were murdered à la Treblinka.

Let's not fool ourselves.

The "Lublin" campaign of November 10–11 also teaches us that once more the Germans have found collaborators and lackeys within the Jewish community.[3] Once again they have found scoundrels to send their brethren off to slaughter with their own hands in order to save their own despicable lives. The gangrene that the

----

[1] SS and Police Chief of the Warsaw District von Sammern and Nazi Ghetto Commissar Auerswald told a *Judenrat* delegation that peace would be restored, that the Ghetto situation had been stabilized and that the Jews should work diligently.

[2] Refers to a new German order to set up several new ghettoes.

[3] The *Judenrat*.

Jewish police and community leaders spread in Warsaw infected shop supervisors who are lowdown outcastes, ready for any infamy.

Don't trust the Jewish bigshots, the shop leaders, or the foremen; they are your enemies. Don't be fooled by them.

Do not allow yourselves to be persuaded that skilled artisans and senior workers with "numbers" are more secure; and only the weaker and defenseless will be extradited.

Everyone is in danger.

Let no one dare aid actively or passively in giving over brother, friend, neighbor, or co-worker to the hangman. As we stand face to face with death let us not be dungheaps or worms, but engage in mutual aid. Traitors that help the enemy must be spewed out of the community.

Do not allow yourselves to be slaughtered like sheep; prepare to defend your lives. Remember that you too—the civilian Jewish population—stand in the forefront of the battle for freedom and humanity.

The enemy has already been heavily wounded. Let us defend our honor.

Let freedom live!

> J.H.I. Ar.
> Ringelblum Ar. II.

17.   WARSAW, JANUARY 2, 1943

Radiogram from Gen. Rowecki to London Concerning Efforts of the Jewish Fighting Organization to Acquire Weapons

Finally Jews from various Communist groups [1] are turning to us for weapons, as though we possess full arsenals. I gave them several pistols on trial but I have no idea whether or not they will use them. I'll give no more arms because, as you know, we don't have them

---

[1] A.K. commander in chief refers to the Jewish Fighting Organization as "Zczydo komuna."

ourselves and are waiting for you to send them to us. Inform me what sort of contact local Jews have with London.

> Kalina
>
> C.Ar. of I.M.
> A.K. Ar.
> Bulletin 1/1124
> *Trans. from Polish*

18. WARSAW GHETTO, JANUARY 13, 1943

SOS Appeal Abroad from Jewish National Committee re Relief and Weapons

New York—Stephen Wise, Goldmann, Workmens Circle, Joint.

We hereby inform you of the greatest crime of all time, annihilation of over three million Polish Jews. Face to face with the threat of murder to the four hundred thousand Jews still alive, we urge you to aid in the following:

1. Revenge on the Germans;
2. Forcing the Nazis to stop the killing;
3. Arms procurement for our fight for life and honor;
4. Maintaining contact through an emissary in neutral countries;
5. Arranging exchange for ten thousand children;
6. Providing $500,000 for self defense and relief.

Brothers! The survivors of the Jews in Poland live with the awareness that in the worst days of our history you have given us no aid. Respond. This is our last appeal to you.

> Jewish National Committee in Poland
>
> C.Ar. of I.M.
> Cable Collection
> SOS Cable 15
> *Trans. from Polish*

19. WARSAW GHETTO, FIRST HALF OF JANUARY 1943

Summons of Jewish Fighting Organization to Active and Passive Resistance

To the Jewish Masses in the Ghetto!

On the 22nd of January 1943, it will be six months since the beginning of the deportations in Warsaw. We remember well the horrifying days in which three hundred thousand of our brothers and sisters were deported and brutally murdered in the Treblinka death camp. Six months have passed in steady terror before death, never knowing about what will happen the next day. Information comes to us from everywhere about exterminating Jews in G.G.,[1] in Germany, and in the occupied countries. Listening to the tragic reports we expect our [end any] moment, day, or hour. Today we must understand that the Nazi murderers let us live only because they want to exploit our labor force till the last [drops] of blood and sweat, till the last breath. We are slaves. When slaves no longer bring profit they are murdered. Each of us must understand and continually remember that fact.

In the last few weeks persons from various [circles] have spread news about letters alleged to have arrived from deported Warsaw Jews in labor camps near Pinsk, or in Bobroisk. Jewish masses, do not believe these tales. They have been spread by Jews in the service of the Gestapo. The bloody murderers are committed to pacifying the Jewish populace in order to facilitate the upcoming deportation and minimize German casualties. They do not want the Jews to prepare hiding places or offer resistance. Jews, don't fall for these lies.

Jewish masses, the hour approaches; you must be prepared to offer resistance and not give yourselves over to slaughter like sheep.

---

[1] *General-Gubernia*—central section of Poland, designated by the Germans as a separate occupied district.

No Jew should climb into the wagon. Persons who have no chance to resist actively should join in passively, i.e., go into hiding. We have just received news from Lemberg that the Jewish police there carried out resettlement of three thousand Jews. In Warsaw that will not happen: the assassination of Lejkin demonstrates this. Our motto: "Be prepared to die like a human being."

> J.H.I. Ar.
> Ringelblum Ar. II
> *Trans. from Polish*

20. WARSAW, JANUARY 1943

Summons of the Farband to Active Rebellion

Prepare for Action! Vigilance!

We are rising to combat!

We have taken on the task of arousing the people. We challenge our community with the slogan: "Wake up and Fight!"

Do not lose hope in deliverance! Know that salvation does not lie in kneeling before death; it lies with something higher, in struggle!

One who fights for his life has a chance to save himself! One who despairs before the fight begins is also finished before the start; his destiny is a humiliating death in the asphyxiation apparatus of Treblinka.

Arise, people, and fight!

Gather courage for bold deeds! Down with shameful submission to a "We are all sentenced to death!" attitude. It has no basis in truth! We too are destined to live. We too have a right to that!

One has to fight for it; it's no trick to live when life is given gracefully! The trick is when someone wants to tear life away.

Arise, my people, and fight for your life!

Let every mother become a lioness defending her children!

Let no father quietly look upon the death of his children! Let there be no repetition of the disgraceful first act of our annihilation!

Let the enemy pay for each Jewish life with its own blood!

Let each of our houses become a fortress!

Rise up, my people, to battle!

Your salvation lies in combat!

Whoever fights for his life has a chance to save himself!

We step forth in the struggle for survival of the helpless masses, to whom we want to bring deliverance, and whom we must inspire to action! Not only for our own lives do we struggle: we save ourselves only when we fulfill our duty! So long as the life of even one Jew remains in danger, we must be on the alert, and struggle!

Our slogan:

Never again shall a Jew perish in Treblinka!

Down with traitors to the people!

Ruthless battle against the occupation till the last drop of our blood!

Be ready for action!

Vigilance!

> J.H.I. Ar.
> Ringelblum Ar. II
> *Trans. from Polish*

21. WARSAW GHETTO, JANUARY 20, 1943

Report on the First Armed Self-Defense

Wednesday, January 20. During the day I am once more at Hashomer. Mordekhai shows me weapons obtained: a rifle and machine gun. We stripped a German policeman of his arms and took the machine gun, and we already know how to use it. Mordekhai reports to me about a struggle at the corner of Zamenhofa and Niska. While walking in a column with other captives, he stood up and led a fight. Several SS were wounded or killed. The others fled, leaving behind their helmets and some weapons. Then the Germans set fire to the house where Mordekhai and others had barricaded themselves. He escaped. I congratulate him on his victory with a comradely handshake.

> Hersz Berlinski: *Memoirs*
> Ar. of J.N.C.

22. WARSAW GHETTO, JANUARY 18, 1943

Appeal by the Jewish Fighting Organization for Active Self-Defense[1]

Jews!

The occupation force has initiated the second stage of your annihilation.

Do not submit to death!

Defend yourselves!

Take up an axe, an iron bar, or a knife in hand; barricade your house. Let them take you that way. Through struggle you have a chance to save yourselves.

Fight!

> J.H.I. Ar.
> Ringelblum Ar. II
> *Trans. from Polish*

23. WARSAW, JANUARY 25, 1943

SOS from Pawel Finder [1] *to Georgy Dimitrov re Armed Self-Defense of the Jews in Warsaw Ghetto, January 18–22, 1943*

From Poland, To Dimitrov.

[. . .] On January 18, the occupation forces proceeded to the final stage of liquidating the Warsaw Ghetto, where 35,000 Jews still live

---

[1] This leaflet was distributed January 18, 1943, as the Germans entered the Ghetto for the final stage of liquidation.

---

[1] After Marceli Nowotko was murdered by the enemy, Pawel Finder (a Jew) became first secretary of P.P.R. Central Committee.

and work for the Germans. This time the Jewish populace, led by our comrades, defended themselves with grenades and stones.[2] The gendarmes were forced to storm several houses. The Ghetto was liquidated. For the moment there is no definitive figure on the [German] murderers' losses.

An indication of the mood in Warsaw can be seen from an appeal printed in the underground newspaper "Nowy Dzien" (favoring Sikorski) to the Delegation. The latter was urged to appeal by radio to England, the United States, and Russia, for thousands of Allied planes to fly over tortured Polish soil, paralyze railroad lines, and force the Germans to deal with defense rather than murder defenseless persons.

Finder

Ar. of Inst. for Party Hist.
Polish Materials in Comintern Ar.
Trans. from Russian

24. WARSAW GHETTO, FEBRUARY 7, 1943

Report to Abroad Concerning Armed Self-Defense of Warsaw Ghetto in January 1943

For Zygelboim.

In January, the Germans moved to liquidate the Warsaw Ghetto, and the populace offered armed resistance. Some tens of Germans were killed and several hundred Jews fell, including our Mermelszteyn, Cholodenko, and Giterman of the Joint Distribution Committee. After three days' resistance the campaign was halted, and six thousand [Jews] were led away.

Throughout Poland liquidation of [the Jews] continues. By mid-February [the Germans] expect to have liquidated the Warsaw

---

[2] The Jewish Fighting Organization led the January self-defense action. Key commanders and fighters there included Mordekhai Anielewicz, Zekariah Artszteyn, Margalit Landau, Benjamin Leibgot, Abraham Feiner, and Itzhak Sukenik.

Ghetto. The whole world is up in arms. The Pope has been approached for official intervention, also the Allies, to declare German prisoners of war as security. We suffer horribly; the surviving two hundred thousand are threatened with annihilation. Only you can save us; posterity will hold you responsible.

> For Central Committee of the Movement of the
>   Jewish Working Masses,[1]
> Janczyn [2] and Berezowski.
>
> Ar. of Inst. for Party Hist.
> Delegation Ar., Cable Collection
> SOS 39

25. WARSAW GHETTO, FEBRUARY 19, 1943

Assault by the Farband upon German Gendarmes in the Ghetto and Setting Fire to SS Warehouse

NEWS RELEASE

On February 18, 1943, an armed assault was carried out on Warsaw Ghetto territory, resulting in the shooting of two German gendarmes.

Tangible gains from the action came in the form of uniforms, a *pistolet* of the "parabellum" type, and a *Wis.* Taking part in the action were nine persons: Pawel,[1] Richard, Monta, Felix, Artur, Janek, Zenon, Michal, and Victor.

PAWEL: SETTING FIRE TO THE SS
WAREHOUSE–A REPORT

On March 6, 1943, an act of sabotage was carried out: setting fire to the SS and police warehouses on Nalewki 31.

[1] Cryptogram for Bund underground.
[2] Maurycy Orzech, killed by the Germans.

---

[1] Pawel Frenkl.

These warehouses, connected with workshops, used to furnish equipment for infirmaries—mattresses, beds, and blankets. Taking part in the action were five specially appointed persons, plus a local group of nine. They used Molotov cocktails, termite bombs, gasoline, and kerosene to burn down their objective.

Both the action itself and the subsequent retreat were orderly, without losses—all before the gendarmes were aroused.

The uniformed German stationed in the area went into hiding as soon as he heard the first two shots, fired in order to frighten him.

Within four minutes four wagons arrived with firemen, five with gendarmes, plus several automobiles with SS, and other police personnel.

The scope of the damage cannot as yet be ascertained. There is no doubt it is substantial.

Commander Zygmund [2]

Collection of Materials of Jewish Military Alliance
(the Farband)
Original copy, from Cesary Ketling
J.H.I. Ar.
Trans. from Polish

26. WARSAW GHETTO, MARCH 3, 1943

Appeal of Jewish Fighting Organization re Carrying Out Death Sentences Against Traitors: Call to Active Struggle

The passive and active resistance of the Jewish masses in the memorable days of January 18–22, 1943, came as a surprise to the Nazi bandits, and convinced them that Jews no longer will go like sheep to slaughter. The Nazi resettlement project has been really disrupted.

The bloody occupation force now knows that through means used thus far it will not destroy the remnants of Warsaw Jewry. Unfortunately, the worst outcasts of the community gave the Ger-

---

[2] Pseudonym of Pawel Frenkl.

mans aid, giving away information on bunkers. These degenerates show the enemy how to liquidate Warsaw Jewry, as has been done in Poniatow and Lublin. In this way, the occupation wishes to uncover and destroy the centers of armed resistance.

After the execution, on February 21, of Gestapo agent Arek Weintraub, a document was found that establishes that he and his "cronies" had recommended to the Germans the plan of "voluntary" and "peaceful" deportation of Jews to Poniatow.

The Gestapo agent Nossig,[1] executed February 22, had provided the Germans with intelligence on Jewish bunkers in attics and cellars. The chief instigator at the *Umschlagplatz,* Brzezinski, executed February 26, was a provocateur within the Fighting Organization and betrayed their representatives to agents.

Well-known Gestapo agent Bobby Nebel, executed February 28, had been involved in spying on the centers of Jewish political life.

Adas Szejn, the editor of the traitorous Gestapo organ "Zagew," [2] executed February 28, was active in informing upon and demoralizing Jewish political life.

The Fighting Organization possesses a complete list of all German lackeys who have forgotten they are Jews and human beings. THE FIGHTING ORGANIZATION WARNS ALL LOW-LIFES THAT IF THEY DO NOT STOP THEIR DEGENERATE DEEDS IMMEDIATELY THEY WILL BE EXECUTED!

We warn all officers and functionaries of the [Jewish] *Ordnungsdienst* not to hinder the activity of Fighting Organization cells; neither chief hangman Brand [3] nor a hideout nor escape to the so-called "Aryan" side can shield against the fighter's bullet.

We warn all shop directors, both in and beyond the Ghetto, not to agitate or try to persuade workers to go to voluntary deportation. Jews!

The German murderers will not ignore you much longer. We

---

[1] Dr. Alfred Nossig, German spy since 1913.

[2] In the first half of 1942 an underground publication issued by assimilationists and Pilsudski cronies appeared in the Warsaw Ghetto; it was called "Zagew." Subsequently, Jewish Gestapo agents issued a sham "Zagew" with diversionary intentions.

[3] Karl-Georg Brand, chief of the Jewish Division of the Warsaw Gestapo.

urge you to unite around the banners of struggle and resistance. Hide your women and children, and present yourselves, with whatever you can, for battle against the Nazi outlaws. The Jewish Fighting Organization counts on your full moral and material support.

> Jewish Fighting Organization

> C.Ar. of I.M.
> Delegation Ar. File 458, p. 255
> *Trans. from Polish*

27. WARSAW GHETTO, MARCH 13, 1943

Letter from Anielewicz to Land Army Command re Weapons for Self-Defense in March

Dear Sirs:

The situation grows worse from one hour to the next. Fifteen hundred persons will be led away today from the Schultz firm. We anticipate a clean-up campaign in the Ghetto and the shops. The brush factory [1] action, in which we succeeded completely, proved to the Germans once and for all that they must revert to methods of siege and brute force. The coming days must bring an end to Warsaw Jewry.

Are we prepared? Materially, very poorly. Only thirty-six of forty-nine pieces of weapons that we've distributed work, because we lack ammunition. Our ammunition reserves have dwindled in frequent actions carried out over the past few weeks. At this point there are at most ten bullets for each gun. This is catastrophic.

I ask that you convey to the authorities [2] in our name that if large-scale aid does not arrive immediately we shall regard that as indifference on the part of the Delegation and the authorities vis-

---

[1] Brush factory workers had sabotaged German deportation orders.
[2] I.e., A.K. leadership.

à-vis the fate of Warsaw Jewry. That we were given arms without ammunition creates the impression of a cynical mockery of our fate, and confirms the impression that the poison of anti-Semitism once more consumes Polish government circles—in utter ignorance of the past three years' experience.

We won't try to convince anyone of our readiness and ability to fight. Beginning January 18, the Jewish community of Warsaw has been in a state of permanent struggle with the occupation and its lackeys. Whoever denies or doubts this is a malicious anti-Semite.

From the authorities and the Delegation we expected not only "understanding" for our cause, but also acknowledgment of the murder of millions of Polish Jewish citizens as their concern too. We regret we have no opportunity for direct contacts with the Allied governments, with the Polish Government, and with Jewish organizations abroad, in order to inform them of our condition and of our treatment at the hands of the authorities and Polish society in general.

Dear Sirs:

I ask you to intercede immediately with the military authority and government Delegation; to read this letter and unequivocally demand immediate delivery of at least one hundred grenades, fifty pistols, ten rifles, and several thousand pieces of ammunition of various calibers. Within two days I am prepared to submit precise plans of our positions, with maps, in order to remove all doubts of our need of weapons.

> Commander of the Jewish Fighting Organization
> ( ) Malacki [3]

At present the situation is tense. In the morning a fighting group attacked two members of the German Police-*Werkschutz* who have been plundering, shooting, and terrorizing the Jewish community for a week, killing and disarming one, shooting the second during

---

[3] Originally written as "Malakhi" (Aniolek, Anielewicz). Typists at the Jewish Division of the A.K. erroneously copied "Malacki" instead of "Malakhi" and after that "Kalacki."

escape. The SA and secret police then marched in and one SA man was heavily wounded. On our side there were no losses.

> J.H.I. Ar.
> Collection of Documents of the Resistance
>   Movement, copies of Anielewicz's letter
> *Trans. from Polish*

28. WARSAW, MARCH 26, 1943

News about Armed Clashes in the Warsaw Ghetto, March 13, 1943

From time to time fighting incidents break out. On March 13, in the morning a Jewish *Werkschutz* [1] was killed, then a German; two Jews were heavily wounded. March 13, on Leszno, two Jews were detained. When they ran away one Jew was killed, two Germans and a Polish agent were wounded. The same day there was revenge shooting in the Ghetto. There are dead.

> "Informacja Biezaca" (Current News) [2]
> No. 12 (85) of March 26, 1943
> *Trans. from Polish*

29. WARSAW, MARCH 20, 1943

Appeal by C. Walter Toebbens [1] Against Resistance Action by the Jewish Fighting Organization

To Jewish armaments workers in the Jewish residential area!
The command of the Fighting Organization posted an appeal the night of March 14, to which I want to respond.

---

[1] A shop watchman.
[2] An information bulletin from A.K. circles.

---

[1] Largest German manufacturer and shop owner in Warsaw Ghetto, SS trustee.

I maintain that

1. There never has been any talk of some non-existent deportation action.
2. Neither Mr. Schultz nor I has been forced to carry out such action under gunpoint.
3. I maintain it is not true that the latest resettlement has failed.

It is unfortunate that workers in the Schultz weapons industry did not wish to listen to the conciliatory suggestions of Mr. Schultz. As a result I regretfully had to intercede by removing a certain workshop in order to utilize the transportation opportunity.

An order has been issued that workers arriving in Trawniki be identified by name so that we may send them their baggage. The claim that travelers in the second convoy from Prosta Street to Poniatow supposedly did not know what was happening with their transport, should be branded as base falsehood and a gross provocation toward weapons industry workers. All members of the convoy are doing well. Since completing the trip they have often travelled back here in trucks with workers and craftsmen in order to take back goods, and so on.

Baggage has not yet been sent from Prosta Street, but is under care of a Jew, Lypszycz, an engineer, who is always ready to provide information about the matter. The baggage will be sent to Poniatow with the next transport. In Trawniki and Poniatow every worker has received his entire baggage and personal effects.

Jewish armament workers! Don't believe those who wish to mislead you. They stir you to the brink of unavoidable consequences.

Neither in the bunkers nor on the Aryan side is there assurance or even a chance of survival. The insecurity alone is sufficient to break down a worker accustomed to regularly functioning on the job. I ask you, why do even wealthy Jews come to me from the Aryan side begging me to take them in with you? They have enough money to live there, but they can't stand it.

With utter sincerity I give you this piece of advice: go to Trawniki and to Poniatow, because there are the living facilities and there you will survive the war!

The Fighting Organization command will not help you, and they offer you merely empty promises. Now they sell you a costly spot in a bunker; later they'll drive you to the streets and leave you to your fate.

You have already suffered enough trickery. Trust only the German factory heads, who, with your cooperation, will maintain production in Poniatow and Trawniki. Bring your wives and children with you; they will also be taken care of.

Walter Toebbens
Plenipotentiary for Problems of Relocating
    Enterprises from the Jewish Quarter in Warsaw

J.H.I. Ar.
Documents of the Brush Factory Administration
Trans. from German [2]

30. WARSAW GHETTO, APRIL 5, 1943

Declaration by Jewish Youth of Its Battle Readiness

LETTER FROM JEWISH YOUTH
TO COMRADES BEYOND THE WALL

As fighters of the Warsaw Ghetto, we too receive the "Walka Mlodych." [1] Over two years have passed since the occupation force isolated us with walls; we greet with joy each fraternal exchange about the struggle against the Germans.

Two months ago our first acquired "hardware" was represented by the axe and bottle of acid. Now we are better armed, as demonstrated on the skins of the fascist hooligans and their Jewish lackeys. We are engaged in perpetual battle; with each day we gain practical experience. A German who enters the Ghetto knows that behind

[2] Toebbens issued this appeal in both German and Polish. Both texts are extant.

[1] Organ of Z.W.M. (Alliance for Young People's Struggle), youth organization of P.P.R.

every wall, in each abandoned house, a fighter's bullet lurks. We never part with weapons. To do so would cost us our lives.

In the rough January days, as SS hooligans massacred the unarmed citizenry in the streets, we drew strength for our struggle from reports that we were not alone, that bombs exploded in Warsaw coffeehouses, that Yugoslavs and other partisans fought well, that in France diversionary activity grows. Hearts warmed with news of the victories of the Red Army, which battles for the liberation of all oppressed.

Comrades, we are with you!

Holding revolvers tightly in hand, we await the moment when together we shall blow up the walls and march out to the ultimate struggle for a free Poland. To all fighters in forests, villages, and cities—a fraternal handshake.

> "Walka Mlodych" (The Battle of Youth)
> No. 4, April 5, 1943
> *Trans. from Polish*

31. WARSAW, APRIL 10, 1943

Notice to London re Danger of Liquidation of Warsaw Ghetto

According to German plan, eight thousand Jewish metal workers are to remain in the Ghetto, plus three thousand workers for *Werterfassung*.[1] All others should be deported or liquidated within two to four weeks. The mood in the Ghetto is tense and despondent.

> Sobol,[2] Kalina
>
> C.Ar. of I.M.
> A.K. Ar., Cable 188
> *Trans. from Polish*

---

[1] German agency for plundering the property of deported and murdered Jews.
[2] Jankowski, Delegation representative in Poland.

32. WARSAW, JANUARY 9–16, 1943

Gen. Rowecki's Announcement Concerning Further Liquidation of Jews

The SS and police chief of Warsaw District issued a command that any Jew found outside the Jewish residential area must be shot immediately without investigation. The creation of provincial ghettoes has turned out to be a pretext to seize and destroy as many Jews as possible. In Otwock, twenty-seven Jews, who presented themselves in the ghetto, were shot immediately. Mass transports arrive once more in Treblinka. From that camp twenty-three carloads of clothing were sent to Germany.

Kalina

C.Ar. of I.M.
A.K. Ar., Cable 175
Trans. from Polish

33. WARSAW, APRIL 12, 1943

News from the Ghetto about Resisting Rebellion in the Ghetto

The heroic resistance, organized by fighting groups for self-defense during the recent campaign in the Warsaw Ghetto, moved the commission on mass murder (so-called *Sonderkommando Umsiedlung)* to stage a new trick. By order of the SS, all active factories in the Ghetto must be evacuated to various spots in the Lublin district, the infamous, tragedy-laden home of Belzec, Trawniki, and Majdanek.

The actual goal of the deportations, aside from economic or military considerations, is to remove Jewish survivors from the metropolitan area with its unlimited possibilities for building hiding places and bunkers, and setting up bases for street fighting.

This time, the murderers, who figured the victims would present themselves willingly, found a surprise. From the fur division of Schultz's factory, marked for deportation, only two hundred out of eight hundred persons offered themselves.

The attempt to evacuate Hallmann's factory crashed. In that great enterprise employing one thousand workers, only fifty-five presented themselves for evacuation. Warehouses containing both lumber and completed furniture designated for military institutions were sent up in flames by a group of Guardists.[1] In the factory area the work of ferreting out Gestapo agents and sabotaging the horrid deportation orders continues.

> Ar. of Inst. for Party Hist.
> Sec. III, "Gwardzista" [2]
> No. 16, April 12, 1943
> *Trans. from Polish*

34. WARSAW GHETTO, APRIL 14, 1943

Appeal of Jewish Fighting Organization re Carrying Out Death Sentence Against a Traitor

For liquidating the Ghetto, Jacob Hirszfeld, manager of Hallmann's shop, was executed on Nowolipie Street. After his execution, posters were distributed in the Ghetto containing the following:

> Jacob Hirszfeld was sentenced to death for inducing the Jewish populace to follow the occupation forces' urgings toward voluntary deportation. Thus did Hirszfeld betray the interests of the Jewish people. His sentence has been carried out; let it be a warning to others.
>
> —THE JEWISH FIGHTING ORGANIZATION

---

[1] Refers to the P.P.R. group of the Jewish Fighting Organization.
[2] Also "Gwardia Ludowa," organ of the People's Guard.

Recently appeals signed by Capt. Jozef Lewicki have appeared on Ghetto walls calling upon Jews to persevere in battle and appealing to the Poles for aid.[1]

> Ar. of Inst. for Party Hist.
> *Trans. from Polish*

35. WARSAW GHETTO, APRIL 1943

Anielewicz's Notes on Moods of the Ghetto Inmates

A CONVERSATION

Several days ago I chatted with a certain resident, an ordinary Jew—not even one of our own. I wanted to sound him out—see how these people think. I began posing questions:

"Nu, how are things?"

"Bitter, my friend! In Cracow a new campaign; in the Lublin district a campaign—soon they'll get to us. . . ."

"So, that'll be the end. . . ."

"What kind of 'end,' my dear sir?" he said. "What happened before won't happen again. This time they won't take us like animals to slaughter."

"Hm . . . that's interesting," I thought, and continued probing, "Today you talk like a bigshot! But what would you do if they came into your neighborhood to take you away?"

"What do you mean 'what would I do?' You wouldn't have to agitate then. I'd get all my friends together; we'd grab axes, iron bars, and hammers and go into cellars or barricade ourselves in the house. Let them come! Let them spray their machine gun bullets left and right. What can they do to me if I'm hidden behind the door? Just let one of them stick his head into the room, and he's mine. Ten of them will fall by my axe. Maybe I'll be the eleventh, but at least that's a way

---

[1] The role of Jozef Lewicki (or according to other sources, Lencki) is not clear. It is assumed he led a diversionary "combat organization," having been instructed by the Gestapo to introduce confusion among the Jewish resistance and in the Ghetto at large.

to die. They will never get us the way they did before! And for them, for our Jewish police, see, my friend, what I have prepared. . . ." He then showed me a long, well-sharpened knife—"God protect anyone starting up with me."

I felt overwhelmed and strengthened. I understood it is still worth struggling. A flame still can be kindled within them. We have inspired a new, proud, strong Jew ready to fight for his life.

FROM ANOTHER CONVERSATION

"What do you mean, they'll take us? It won't be so easy. We'll arm ourselves with axes, then let them take us. Let them throw grenades and bombs, let them plant mines and dynamite—that's how they'll have to get us. For deportation we aren't going to go out into the street. If one of them comes inside, he won't get out alive. If somebody smells me out in a hiding place I'll keep on fighting; it's him or me. If I have to die it'll be like a human being, not a sheep in a pen."

TO YOU

Let us rise up en masse, in the thousands, in one camp. Whoever you are and however you think, if you possess a proud soul and a heart unpoisoned by the dirt of the street, join us. Stand shoulder to shoulder to fight for survival of the helpless, doomed masses.

J.H.I. Ar.
Ringelblum Ar. II
Trans. from Polish

36. CRACOW, APRIL 20, 1943

Letter from Gov. Gen. Frank to Lammers [1]
Concerning Outbreak of the Warsaw Ghetto Uprising

Since yesterday there has been a well-organized uprising in the Ghetto, which we must counteract with the aid of cannon.

> Ar. of High Commission to Investigate Nazi War
>   Crimes in Poland
> Record of Biller's Trial, vol. II, p. 33
> *Trans. from German*

37. WARSAW, APRIL 20, 1943

First Report of SS Gen. Stroop re Outbreak of Fighting in the Warsaw Ghetto

DISPATCH

Sender: SS and Police Chief of Warsaw District,
    Warsaw, 20 April 1943

Sign: 1 A'B = st/gr. 1607. N'R 43/516 secret.

To: Higher SS and Police Chief "East," Cracow

Course of action in the Ghetto, April 19, 1943. Ghetto was sealed off at 0300 hrs. At 0600 hrs., *Waffen SS* attacked using a 16/850 [1] ratio. The goal was to wipe out the so-called rump-Ghetto.
Immediately after entry of our troops came a strong, well-planned fire attack from the Jews and outlaws. The tank and three

---

[1] Chief of Hitler's chancellery.

[1] 850 enlisted men and 16 officers.

armored vehicles introduced into the battle were then bombed with Molotov cocktails (incendiary bottles).[2] The tank was twice set on fire. Our troops had to retreat. Losses in the first attack: twelve persons (six SS men and six Trawniki men).[3] About 0800 hrs., the second attack by our army unit took place, led by the undersigned. Despite more resistance by fire, our offensive was effective in clearing out the building complexes. The enemy has pulled back from attic and rooftop battle stations into cellars, bunkers, and sewers. During the cleanup nearly two hundred Jews were seized. The SA was issued an order to attack known bunkers, drag out those in hiding, and destroy the bunkers. In this way, nearly 380 Jews were captured. It has been established that Jews are hiding in sewers. All sewers have been flooded with water, in order to make hiding there impossible. At 1700 hrs., we met strong resistance from a house group that defended itself with automatic weaponry.[4] A special combat group overwhelmed the enemy and broke into the houses, but captured no one. The Jews and criminals defended themselves, going from one defense point to the next, and at the last moment slipped away, escaping through attics and underground passages.

Around 2000 hrs., units encircling the Ghetto were relieved and sent to their quarters. Their places were taken by 250 men of *Waffen SS.*

CONTINUATION OF THE CAMPAIGN: APRIL 20

Forces under our command:

SS Armored grenadiers, Reserve Battalion, 6/400;
SS Cavalry, Reserve Battalion, 10/450;
Ordnungspolizei, 6/165;

---

[2] At the corner of Mila and Zamenhofa.

[3] Ukrainian and Latvian Fascists and ordinary Germans from the SS training school in the Trawniki concentration camp.

[4] On Muranowska Street.

Sicherheitsdienst, 2/48;
Trawniki men, 1/150;
Wehrmacht:
   One 10 cm. Howitzer, 1/7;
   One flame thrower, 1;
   Pioneers,[5] 2/16
   Sanitary groups, 1/1;
   Three 2.28 cm. anti-aircraft artillery, 2/24;
   One French armored wagon of *Waffen SS;*
   Two tanks of *Waffen SS.*

   Total: 31/1262

I have turned over command for today's campaign to Schups-major Sternhagen, who will receive further orders from me.

At 0700 hrs. nine Storm detachments were thrown into battle in a ratio of 1/36 with various types of weaponry, to carry out a precise search of the so-called rump-Ghetto. The search is still in progress; the first stage should be over at 1100 hrs. In the meantime, it has been established that in the uninhabited or as yet unevacuated Ghetto, with its weapons factories and the like, there is a substantial number of nests of resistance. They even pushed back a tank that was in the Ghetto.[6]

Two combat detachments have overwhelmed these resistance nests and thus cleared the way for the tanks. Two *Waffen SS* have been wounded.

In comparison with yesterday, the opposition is acting more cautiously, obviously impressed by our heavy arms.

I intend to comb through the so-called rump-Ghetto and thus wipe out the allegedly uninhabited parts. Meanwhile, it has been verified that in that Ghetto area there are still to be found at least ten to twelve bunkers, some of them in weapons factories; these factories

[5] Sappers.
[6] On Smocza Street.

with their machines and tools must be put under protection, because of the danger of shooting and fires.

The next report will arrive this evening.

> SS and Police Chief in Warsaw District STROOP
> SS Brigadier General and Police Major General
> Report validated by SS Major JESUITER

> From Stroop's Report File
> Ar. of High Commission to Investigate Nazi War Crimes in Poland
> *Trans. from German*

38. WARSAW, APRIL 20, 1943

Report of the Outbreak of the Ghetto Uprising: Between Ghetto Walls, Under Blue-and-White and Red-and-White Banners

Twenty thousand Warsaw Jews are being wiped out in a desperate battle. Storm battalions, armored cars, and airplanes take part in the bloody Ghetto expedition. A group of Jews has escaped through a break in the chain. From Sunday on, events enacted in the Warsaw Ghetto would be called horrible by any civilized person. The Germans are moving to finish off the twenty thousand Jews still remaining in Warsaw. Here is an account of events as the Jews offer desperate armed resistance.

Sunday, 2:00 P.M., the German police received an order to proceed relentlessly toward ultimate liquidation of the Warsaw Ghetto. At a consultation session at SS and police headquarters the battle plan was laid. Some 400 German police were designated for the action, plus 420 Polish police to guard the blockade around the Ghetto. About 6:00 P.M., they began surrounding the Ghetto, and the Jews, aware of the danger that faced them, offered armed resistance.

Sunday night, bitter fighting took place. Attacking gendarmes were pelted with grenades and shot at with revolvers, causing many German casualties. In the morning, the Germans brought in help—three SS battalions, plus armored cars and artillery. From 5:00 A.M., heavy fusillades and incessant explosions were heard. Conquering the barricaded buildings, especially ones where the stairs had been blown away, was particularly difficult. The Germans destroyed many buildings with artillery and set fire to others; they even used airplanes to drop fire bombs, enveloping the Ghetto in clouds of smoke. Ignoring this [the Jews] continued their bitter, heroic resistance. At certain buildings, e.g., at Muranowski Square 4, the Zionist blue-and-white flag was hung and next to it, the Polish flag.

Monday about 6:00 P.M., unexpected help came to the Jews from the Polish part of the city. A fighting detachment broke through the German chain in the area of Krasinski Square and gave a group of Jews a chance to escape;[1] however, in the course of the evening Jewish resistance weakened, and appears now to have been broken.[2] The Germans are completing the bloody job of shooting on the spot hundreds of captured Jews, including women and children. The Polish police had already pulled out yesterday.[3]

"Nowy Dzien" [4]
No. 546, April 20, 1943
Trans. from Polish

39. WARSAW, APRIL 22, 1943

Report on Polish, Jewish, and Soviet Flags of the Ghetto Fighters

Large numbers of Polish onlookers gawked at the fighting [in the Ghetto], a number of whom were killed or wounded by stray bullets. The Germans in no instance disturbed the crowd.

---

[1] Refers to either the attack by People's Guard on Nowiniarska Street not far from Krasinski Square, or the appearance of the A.K. group on Sapiezynska Street. More about that later.

[2] A false impression.

[3] Incorrect—the Polish police remained.

[4] A Polish underground newspaper published by a group of Democratic journalists. Same as "Dzien."

The Jews hung out numerous flags—Polish and Jewish with the Shield of David. A Polish one with an embroidered Soviet emblem was also observed. There were also signs carrying the appeal: "Poles, help us." The commanders of resistance groups are apparently the Soviet parachutists of Jewish nationality.[1]

> Ar. of Inst. for Party Hist.,
> Sec. III, Delegation Materials,
> Interior Dept. Report 153
> *Trans. from Polish*

40.　WARSAW, MAY 10, 1943

Report on the Red and Blue-and-White Flags of the Uprising—Participation of the Communists

According to reliable information there existed in the Ghetto an organization built on the system of "fives," and headed by a Jewish major of the Polish Army.[1] This was not the only such organization there, because during the first six days of the battle both Zionist and red flags appeared in the Ghetto area. In any case, both organizations were able to build up a large reserve of ammunition, apparently with Communist help.

From the German side appeared detachments of gendarmes, SS, and Shaulists. The Polish police joined in the battle voluntarily. Our informant observed a group of approximately fifty police.

During the course of the fighting our observer noticed a group of Jews standing at a window of a burning building, apparently quite calm. When the conflagration intensified, firefighters urged them to leave the building. They refused even after the second call. When their apartment began burning, a man with a child jumped from the

---

[1] Probably based on Pinya Kartin (Andrzej Schmidt) having served as first commander of the Anti-Fascist Bloc (May–March 1942) upon arrival from Moscow as a parachutist.

---

[1] Anieléwicz received a major's title; other staff members, captain.

window; after him, the others. German artillery stood by on the grounds of Weigl's factory (that would be burned later). These fires were set by the Germans in the neighborhood of Muranowska and subsequently spread. The Jews from their side set fire to manufacturing firms in the Ghetto region.

The Jews were spreading propaganda that "people from the forest" [2] would come to the aid of the Ghetto if the resistance lasts two weeks. The idea was widely accepted especially in the Little Ghetto, but no help has yet arrived. The Polish police fire at those who try to escape.

The occupation has let out word about increased responsibility for Poles helping Jews. The leadership of Civil War [3] has released a communiqué urging Poles to aid the hiding Jews, full-fledged citizens of Poland. Polish informers will be punished by death. Many cases are known of such death sentences having been carried out. Distribution of this communiqué has been poor and we know many instances of informing by uninvolved [Poles].

The masses stare at the battle out of plain curiosity.

"Czyn" (The Deed) [4]
No. 2, May 10, 1943.
Trans. from Polish

41. WARSAW, APRIL 20, 1943

SOS to London re Outbreak of Ghetto Uprising

For Zygelboim and Szwarczbard.[1]

On April 19, the SS detachments with tanks and artillery began exterminating the remnants of the Warsaw Ghetto. The Ghetto

---

[2] Partisans.

[3] A Delegation institution.

[4] Organ of the "Syndicalists" (former Z.Z.Z., Pilsudski-oriented trade unions of Moraczewski).

---

[1] Dr. Itzhak Szwarczbard, former Sejm deputy, representative of the General Zionists in the National Council of the Polish government-in-exile in London.

offers a heroic armed resistance. Leading the self-defense is the Jewish Fighting Organization, which has concentrated almost all factions [2] within its structure. From the Ghetto come steady fusillades and heavy explosions; airplanes circle the grounds of the massacre. The outcome of the battle was sealed before the start. Evenings, a flag hangs over Ghetto-fighters' positions with the inscription: "We'll fight to the end."

Heavy tension covers the city. Admiring Warsaw residents follow the fighting with obvious friendship for the embattled Ghetto.

We urge immediate acts of revenge. Demand that International Red Cross visit the ghettoes, Auschwitz, Treblinka, Belzec, Sobibor, Majdanek, and the other death camps in Poland.

> For Central Committee of the Movement of Jewish
>   Working Masses
> Berezowski
>
> For the Jewish National Committee
> Borowski [3]
>
> Ar. of Inst. for Party Hist.
> Delegation Materials, Cable
> *Trans. from Polish*

42. WARSAW, APRIL 23, 1943

SOS from Pawel Finder [1] to Dimitrov re Outbreak of Ghetto Uprising

To Dimitrov:

On April 18, the Germans moved to liquidate the Warsaw Ghetto, and Jews answered with armed resistance. Three days and three nights of battle have ensued. Detachments of SS gendarmes, Shaulists (detachments of armed Lithuanian Fascists), and Ukrain-

---

[2] Akiva, Gordonia, Hechalutz, Hanoar Hatzioni, Hashomer Hatzair, Jewish Labor Bund, Left Labor Zionists, P.P.R., and Right Labor Zionists.

[3] Dr. Adolph (Abraham) Berman.

---

[1] Secretary General of Central Committee of P.P.R.

ians began a siege with the aid of mine throwers, artillery tanks, and armored cars. Yesterday explosive and fire bombs dropped from airplanes. The Jews defend themselves heroically with all their might, to the degree permitted by the number of weapons (grenades, machine guns, and pistols). Ammunition reserves are dwindling.

Among the Germans and Shaulists there are hundreds of dead and wounded. Our Polish groups are carrying out diversionary attacks from the outside on gendarmes and SS, and have killed several Germans.

Finder

Ar. of Inst. for Party Hist.
Polish Comintern Materials
Trans. from Russian

43. WARSAW GHETTO, APRIL 20, 1943

Fragment of Marysia's Diary on Outbreak of the Warsaw Ghetto Uprising

Yesterday a truly bloody battle erupted in the Ghetto. Tanks, cannon, and heavy machine guns were moved into the Ghetto, and unmerciful battle was declared upon the Jews who dared raise their heads a bit in return for Treblinka, Belzec, Trawniki, and for the entire hell we live through. From morning powerful explosions are heard, echoes of revolver shots, the rattle of machine guns, and the whole symphony of sounds that blend into one little word pregnant with the blood of the murdered, revenge, and the clash of enemy forces—the word FIGHT.

The Ghetto has arisen. The Ghetto has arisen. All told, only several hundred men [1] armed with revolvers have stood up to battle the hangman, poised to protect what remains of human dignity. The great and glorious hour of the future has struck because the survivors of misfortune, degradation, and gruesome torture, fashioned by the

[1] Organized rebels apparently numbered over a thousand men and women. The spontaneous groups that participated in the fighting numbered in the thousands.

fantasy of a madman who rules the world, have dared to straighten their spines. . . .

The siege of the Ghetto has lasted two days. Tanks, cannon, automatic weaponry, and the whole array of modern murder-technology has been introduced into the battle by the beast of the twentieth century. The massacre has lasted two days, leaving behind on the field of death ruins and bodies. Until now, I've had no way to ascertain the number of losses on both sides.

One fact stands clear: many gendarmes have fallen. It has even been reported that the ratio of casualties between Germans and Jews as of noon on the first day of fighting was fifty-two to twenty-eight. Against tanks, cannon, and machine guns stood five hundred to eight hundred men armed with revolvers. I probably do not have to add that the battle ended in our defeat and that the Germans, drunk with their first victory in two years march triumphant with song on their lips, "When Jewish Blood Spurts from the Knife."

> Ar. of Majdanek Museum
> *Marysia's Diary*
> *Trans. from Polish*

44. WARSAW, APRIL 21, 1943

Order to Deport Jewish Workers from the Warsaw Ghetto

To the Management of the Following Firms:

Schultz & Co., Inc.
Karl-Georg Schultz & Co.
Bernard Hallmann & Co.
Oskar Schilling & Co.
Herrestandartverwaltung [1]
W. von Schoen
Leszczynski

---

[1] German military expropriator of brush factory production.

E. Welk
G. Gerlach
Julian Kudasiewicz [2]
W.C. Toebbens
W. Hoffmann
Oksako Share Co.
Kurt Rerich, Inc.
Hermann Breuer
Ostdeutsche Bau-Tischlerei, Inc.[3]

By authority of SS and Police Chief of Lublin District, SS Maj. Gen. and Lt. Gen. of Police Globocnik, in accordance with order no. 5423/43/011 dated March 12, 1943, and with the consent of SS and Police Chief of Warsaw District, SS Brig. Gen. and Maj. Gen. of Police Stroop, I inform you of the following:

1. Transfer of the Jewish labor force will take place April 21, 1943. Marching begins 6:00 A.M.
2. Transfer of materials and machinery will be carried out according to my instructions.
3. Jewish workers may continue to take with them personal effects. Maximum weight: 15 kilograms per person.
4. The management is responsible for two days' meals.
5. Several police detachments are at your disposal for the operation. I shall assign them to the factories 6:00 P.M. this evening. The latter are responsible for their board.
6. In order to assure transfer of material and machinery, a small number of Jewish labor squads will remain in Warsaw with special identifications cards approved by SD.
   a. Workers from the W.C. Toebbens firm (at Courthouse Street) and that of Karl-Georg Schultz will gather at the side of the street adjacent to the sealed-off area.
   b. Workers from Schultz & Co., Bernard Hallmann & Co.,

---

[2] Polish co-proprietor of the brush factory.
[3] Located on Gesia Street and managed by Alexander Landau, a resistance sympathizer.

Oskar Schilling & Co., and Kurt Rerich will present themselves for transit at Nowolipie Street.

c. Herman Breuer employees will gather in the yard at the firm's factory building at Nalewki 38.

d. Workers under the military authority and Messrs. E. Welk, G. Gerlach, and Julian Kudasiewicz should gather at the factory yard at Swietnojerska 32.

e. Employees of the W. von Schoen firm should gather at the factory yard on Chicken Street.[4]

I hereby categorically inform the factory managements that workers found after resettlement in the sealed off district, without proper identification will be shot according to military law.

f. I hereby urge factory managements to concern themselves with carrying through the final transfer and thereby secure the materials and machinery.

g. This measure has been taken because, with difficulties recurring daily, no other solution seems feasible.

Walter C. Toebbens

J.H.I. Ar.
Files of Brush Factory Office
Trans. from German

45. WARSAW GHETTO, APRIL 21–26, 1943

Report of Battles on Nowolipie and Nowolipki

...[1] who dragged themselves along the whole of Nowolipie towards the main building of the firm, in order not to miss the "privilege" of being deported to Trawniki. Their eyes screamed hunger, terror, and despair: Schultz's emissaries had brought the

---

[4] Berish Majzels Street, or Kupiecka.

---

[1] The beginning of the document was so damaged as to be illegible.

good news to the bunker, that somehow all bunkers would be un-covered—either through the ample supply of Jewish informers or simply because all Ghetto buildings were in any case to be razed. Hunger, confusion, and resignation drove thousands of persons to present themselves for deportation to Trawniki. They were followed by the ironical, contemptuous stares of the SS men, who kept silent—why provoke a victim submitting to his own slaughter. . . .

On [April 23], SS men burned down so-called wild buildings on Nowolipie 8 from which, the day before, bullets had fallen on the heads of the German patrols stationed along the length of the wall at Nowolipki. Jewish combat groups, from their side, burned down [the German] warehouse on Pawia and Smocza. The flames that raged there all night illuminated adjacent buildings.

On [April] 24, the action was continued although there remained only 1,200 persons in the whole area, including 230 so-called legal [employees and officials] of the firm.

Gen. Stroop's visit to the area came as quite a surprise to res-idents. Stroop arrived with an entourage including a bodyguard of scores of SS men armed from head to toe. The general already declared that he cared nothing for the value of the warehouses and was prepared to destroy them all if they perhaps concealed a Jew.

Judging further fighting pointless, Jewish combat groups began retreating from the area. A twenty-five-person Fighting Organiza-tion squad was the first to leave. On the way out, it met a German group coming to demolish a bunker at Nowolipie 30. The latter blocked the Jews from breaking out of the area at Karmelicka 15. The Germans opened fire, but at the same moment a grenade fell on them from the roof of Nowolipki 23 and raised a big cloud of smoke and dust. With the Germans forced to shoot blindly, the Fighting Organization squad was able to escape without casualties.

The campaign to unmask bunkers continued through the 25th and 26th, but the purpose of this later activity was mainly to plunder abandoned dwellings, because streets had already been emptied and the number of those in hiding negligible, and . . .

J.H.I. Ar.
Fodkanski–Kaszniec Files
Trans. from Polish

46.   WARSAW, APRIL 28, 1943

Report on Solidarity Battle Action by People's Guard at the Ghetto Walls: April 20–23, 1943

FROM "LIFE AND STRUGGLE IN
WARSAW—SOLIDARITY BATTLE ACTIONS"

In a series of military actions, Polish Warsaw has displayed its solidarity with embattled Jewry. We received the information on these moves from the People's Guard command.

On April 20 at 1:45,[1] a People's Guard squad, named for Warynski, attacked a large enemy machine-gun nest on Nowiniarska, killing the entire crew consisting of two *Waffen SS* men and two of their Polish police lackeys standing in the rear. The attackers got away without casualties.

On April 22, at 4:05, another People's Guard group destroyed the railroad tracks between the bridge and eastside railway station. This together with another action, where railroad cars used for military transport between the westside and central railroad stations were set afire, disrupted railroad traffic in Warsaw for two days.

On April 23, another People's Guard group assaulted a truck with gendarmes on Freta Street. The vehicle had pulled up before a building there. The gendarmes climbed out, took possession of the gateway, and moved on inside. Four gendarmes and the driver stayed inside the truck; one gendarme took up a position at the gate. Guardists threw two grenades, one of which hit the truck roof and bounced to the pavement; the second fell inside the vehicle setting it on fire. Two gendarmes shot blindly into a crowd. German losses: five killed, one vehicle destroyed. The Guard squad not only suffered no casualties, but also succeeded in shooting to death several gendarmes and Polish policemen at the Ghetto gates.

[1] Document does not specify A.M. or P.M.—*trans.*

Obviously, every armed force in Warsaw is capable of carrying out such actions; unfortunately, however, most military leaders, even in the face of blatant German criminality, would rather procrastinate, their "weapons at their feet." [2] The notion of so-called limited warfare advocated by the Polish reactionaries has been proved bankrupt.

> "Glos Warszawy" [3] (Voice of Warsaw)
> No. 21 (30), April 28, 1943
> *Trans. from Polish*

47. LONDON, APRIL 22, 1943

Program on Radio Station "Swit" [1]
about the Ghetto Uprising

The heroic struggle of the Warsaw Ghetto continues. A series of well-fortified positions is still holding out. Jewish combat groups display much battle experience. The leader of the Jewish Labor Bund, the engineer Michael Klepfisz, member of the top resistance cadre, died a glorious hero's death on a glorious battlefield.

48. WARSAW, APRIL 23, 1943

Appeal by the Jewish Fighting Organization
to the Polish Population [1]

Poles, citizens, soldiers for freedom!

Amidst resounding cannon, the German Army bombards our houses and dwellings of our mothers, wives, and children; amidst the crack of machine guns we seized from gendarmes and SS men; amidst the smoke and conflagration and blood of the murdered

---

[2] Refers to A.K. leadership.
[3] Publication of the Warsaw branch of P.P.R.

---

[1] The station was located at the edge of London.

---

[1] Written on the Aryan side by Jewish Labor Bund activist Itzhak Samsonowicz.

Warsaw Ghetto, we, the Ghetto captives, address ourselves to you with fraternal greetings.

We know you look at the war we have waged the past few days against the occupation force through pain and tears, with amazement and fear for the outcome of this struggle. You will soon have the opportunity to see every doorway in the Ghetto transformed into a fortress. We may all perish in battle, but we will not give up. We, like you, passionately lust to avenge the crimes committed by our common enemy. This is a struggle for our freedom and yours; for our human, social, and national honor, and yours!

We will take revenge for Auschwitz, Treblinka, Belzec, and Majdanek.

Long live the brotherhood of arms and blood of embattled Poland!

Long live freedom!

Death to the murderous and criminal occupation!

Let the life and death struggle against the German occupation prosper!

> Jewish Fighting Organization
> *Trans. from Polish*

49. MOSCOW, MAY 18, 1943

Program over Radio Station "Kosciuszko" with an Appeal to Aid the Embattled Ghetto

The Warsaw Ghetto has been embroiled in an heroic life-and-death struggle for almost a month. Words do not suffice to pay the homage due the remaining thirty-five thousand Jews there for the heroic dedication with which they resist the attacks of an overwhelmingly powerful opponent, Hitler's murderous beasts. The Nazis used the latest death tools—tanks, airplanes, and artillery, in order to choke off an insurrection by a handful of people wasted by hunger, mercilessly executed by Hitler's hangmen.

But this time the enemy encountered a resistance that they never expected from their victims. Cannon and heavy artillery did not help them; nor the hundreds of demolition and thousands of incendiary bombs they hurled at the unfortunate Ghetto.

Hundreds of buildings have been turned to ruins by bombs, and under the ruins lay buried hundreds, even thousands, of persons. Conflagrations rage in the Ghetto, and in the sea of flames flowing between the buildings, men, women, and children grit their teeth and do battle. They greet the Nazi murderers with rifles and volleys of machine-gun fire; they rain down stones and bricks upon the enemy. They fight with axe and stick and throw themselves upon the German hangman with their bare hands, trying to shield their families and children. Ghetto dwellers fight to the last drop of blood, exacting a high price for their lives. Thousands of Nazi murderers already lie dead in the streets of the Ghetto; even more of these German scoundrels have been wounded. Despite their overwhelming resources, the Nazis have not broken the heroic resistance of Ghetto residents. How marvelous has been the courage, boldness, and dedication they have displayed in recent weeks.

Warriors of the Polish underground and soldiers of the People's Guard have come to the aid of the Ghetto defenders, spraying their fire upon the German murderers and their lackeys. Thanks to this aid thousands of armed Jews have broken out of the Ghetto and made their way to the forests, where they reinforce Polish partisan groups. However, support from other factions in Warsaw and the country at large has been weak. Armed solidarity acts are still insignificant when compared with the scope of fighting in the Ghetto itself. [. . .] It is critical, now, to set in motion the broadest possible solidarity action with the Ghetto dwellers. Our Polish national honor, especially the honor of the Polish working class, demands this. When czarist satraps tried instigating pogroms against Jews in Warsaw in 1906, they encountered resistance by workers determined to rebuff the "Black Hundred."

At the moment that the month of heroism of our fellow citizens, the Jews of Warsaw, draws to an end, we turn to the people of Warsaw and the entire country with an appeal: Rush to the aid of the heroic Ghetto fighters! Organize a mass solidarity struggle! Attack the Nazi murderers with weapons in hand! Do not permit them to murder the defenders of the Ghetto! Help the Ghetto dwellers free themselves; set up hiding places for them; help them join the ranks of Polish partisans.

Let the heroic struggle of the Warsaw Ghetto inmates once more remind us that only a determined armed resistance can upset the demonic machinations of the Nazi bandits, prevent their murdering, and bring us the liberation.

Death to all Nazi murderers!

Long prosper the joint solidarity struggle of Poles and Jews against the German killers!

> Ar. of Inst. for Party Hist.
> Sec. III, 321, File 34, pp. 641–43
> *Trans. from Polish*

50. WARSAW, APRIL 28, 1943

SOS from Jewish Communal Delegates to London, Demanding Immediate Relief

Attention Zygelboim and Szwarczbard:

The Warsaw Ghetto has been battling heroically for nine days. Against 40,000 Jews [the Germans] use artillery, flamethrowers, and incendiary bombs dropped from airplanes. They demolish housing blocks with mines. The Ghetto is ablaze; clouds of smoke envelop the city. Women and children are burned alive. Sewer exits have been sealed off and are guarded by German patrols.

Our fighters, struggling bitterly, deliver the enemy some heavy blows, setting fire to German factories and weapons industry arsenals. German dead and wounded number one thousand. The bearing of the fighters amazes civilians and draws shame and anger from the Germans. An appeal has been issued by the Jewish Fighting Organization to the inhabitants of the capital. In an appeal of their own, the Polish workers' parties pay tribute to the fighters.

The Allies could really provide immediate, tangible aid. In the name of millions of Jews already murdered, in the name of those now being burned and slaughtered, in the name of those fighting heroically, and in the name of all of us who have been sentenced to death, we appeal to the entire world:

Now, not in the murky future! Let the bloodthirsty enemy feel Allied might now. Let everyone know that revenge is being taken.

Let our closest allies finally take cognizance of their responsibility for Hitler's crimes against an entire people and the tragic epilogue now being played out. Let the heroic, historically singular struggle of the Ghetto inmates at last arouse the world to deeds equal to the greatness of the moment.

> Berezowski,[1] for the Central Committee of the Jewish Working Masses in Poland
>
> Borowski, for the Jewish National Committee
>
> Ar. for Inst. of Party Hist.
> Delegation Files, Cable 81
> *Trans. from Polish*

51. WARSAW GHETTO, APRIL 28, 1943

Letter from Mordekhai Anielewicz to Comrades on the Aryan Side

This is the eighth day of our fight for life. The night of April 19, the Warsaw Ghetto—one of the last—was suddenly surrounded by regular German forces on the way to liquidating surviving Jews. Subsequently, in the first few days, the Germans suffered many losses and were forced to retreat from the Ghetto. Then, with the aid of tanks, armored cars, cannon, and even airplanes, they proceeded formally to besiege the Ghetto and systematically set buildings afire. The number of casualties—men, women, and children—victims of mass execution or burning has been phenomenal. Our days are numbered, yet so long as we possess bullets we shall fight and defend ourselves.

---

[1] Cryptonym of the Jewish Labor Bund underground.

We have rejected the German ultimatum urging us to surrender, because the enemy, knowing no mercy, leaves us no alternative. As time runs out, we demand that you remember how we've been betrayed; there will come a day of reckoning for our sacred, spilt blood. Send relief to those who will escape the enemy's grip before the final hour, so they may continue the struggle.

> Ar. of J.N.C.
> (in possession of Dr. A. Berman [Tel Aviv])
> *Trans. from Hebrew*

52. WARSAW, APRIL 26, 1943

P.P.R. Intelligence Report on the Ghetto Struggle and German Casualties [1]

1. Last Thursday, the Jewish combat squads tried unsuccessfully to seize Pawiak Prison, and lost twenty men.[2]

2. Last Friday, radio station "Swit" issued a bulletin on the fighting in the Warsaw Ghetto and appealed to London and Moscow to bomb Berlin.

3. In the first two days, the Germans estimated their losses in the Ghetto at 150 killed, and through Good Friday, 700 dead and wounded. SS contingents at Grochow have lost 70 men, including the commander.

4. On Holy Thursday, a Soviet observation plane flew over Warsaw.

5. Despite the cutoff there is still water in the Ghetto, albeit flowing weakly, in ground floors and cellars; total cutoff of water supply was impossible. Electricity has not been turned off. The Germans have demolished a number of sewer exits to prevent con-

---

[1] This information was gathered by the intelligence department of the P.P.R. from German sources.

[2] This claim, unconfirmed by Jewish sources, was grossly exploited by the Polish underground press; it was highly exaggerated fantasy to claim the Jews could have taken the prison. The document does at least attest to an unsuccessful attack on Pawiak.

tact with the Aryan side. This has caused heavy damage and sewer problems all over Warsaw.

6. In Zoliborz, a leaflet was distributed carrying a greeting to Poles from the Jewish proletariat, "fighting for our and your freedom."

7. At dawn Friday, a vehicle with mostly young Jewish women and one man, arrived at Mokotowy Prison, followed by another vehicle, containing SS men. In Powonzek,[3] Jewish women were loaded onto streetcars and where taken, no one knows. Today a freight train waits on tracks in Powonzek, its sixteen cars filled with Jews. The Jews beg their Latvian SS guards for water; some of them bribe the guards. . . .

11. Last week SS officers ordered two thousand copies of a map of the Jewish quarter from the Zambrowski firm.

Ar. of Inst. for Party Hist.
Sec. III, Files of P.P.R.
Central Committee Intelligence 233, Bulletin 41
Trans. from Polish

53. WARSAW, APRIL 20, 1943

Portrayal of Ghetto Fighting in Central Organ of the A.K.: April 19–27, 1943

DEFENSE OF THE WARSAW GHETTO

On Monday, the 19th of this month, the German police, armed with light machine guns, closed in on the Ghetto. At dawn, truckloads of hundreds of SS men arrived from two directions, Nalewki and Stawki; their goal was to wipe out the main Ghetto with its forty thousand registered and equal number of unregistered Jews.

Just as the SS were about to load the train at Stawki with Jews, shots and grenades began to rain down upon them: the Jewish

---

[3] A suburb to the north of Warsaw, not far from the Ghetto.

Fighting Organization had begun defense of the Ghetto. What had begun as individual acts of self-defense was now turning into an organized campaign.[1] A regular street battle broke out, reaching its climax Monday night. Several score Germans were killed, especially SS men, and many were wounded. Both sides used machine guns, rifles, grenades, and revolvers. The Jews carried out several attacks that even resulted in casualties beyond the Ghetto walls. For example, at the intersection of Bonifraterska and Konwiktorska streets they completely exterminated a five-man German police patrol.[2]

The fighting continued on Tuesday and lasted through Thursday with the [now] more-cautious Germans introducing some tanks, field artillery, anti-tank artillery, and even observer planes into the foray. The aim of German strategy was to loosen the fighting groups and positions; they also resorted to setting extensive fires and turning off the water supply as a means of breaking the resistance. The Jews, in turn, began setting fire to warehouses of raw materials and finished goods, factories, and tanneries, thus sending up in smoke the vast resources the Germans had accumulated in the Ghetto. Today, the Ghetto is wrapped in flames and clouds of smoke.

The night of the 22nd of this month, a group of Jews tried to break out of the Ghetto at Wolnoszcz Street,[3] but German submachine-gun fire made the escape impossible. During the fighting on the 23rd, [the Jews], according to unconfirmed reports, destroyed several German tanks. The number of casualties has multiplied. In the evening, a bomb was thrown under a German vehicle on Freta Street,[4] killing several SS men and two civilians.

Saturday, the 24th, organized collective self-defense broke down, leaving only scattered resistance groups deep in the Ghetto.[5] The

---

[1] In reality the opposite took place: the collective effort inspired a wave of individual acts of resistance.

[2] This was actually a Land Army assault. Characteristically, the A.K. official organ did not admit A.K. participation, but listed the action as a Jewish effort—so intensively was contact with Jews rejected.

[3] At the periphery of the Ghetto near the cemetery at Okopowa and Gesia.

[4] Once more the central A.K. organ refuses to acknowledge Polish involvement in the action—leftists, at that—the People's Guard.

[5] Incorrect; on April 27, two major battles took place at Ghetto border points, at Leszno Street and Muranowski Square.

Germans have begun gathering the Jews at the *Umschlagplatz* for deportation.

Heavy echoes of the fighting were heard on the 25th, 26th, and 27th of this month. Flames rage with mounting intensity, yet Ghetto defense continues.

> Ar. of Inst. for Party Hist.
> Sec. III, "Bulletin Informacyjny"
> No. 17 (172), April 29, 1943
> *Trans. from Polish*

54. WARSAW, APRIL 28, 1943

Report on German Losses

... the street fighting proves that the Jewish resistance cannot be broken, and will last several weeks at least. The defenders have barricaded themselves in the buildings, having transformed them into fortresses connected by underground tunnels used as routes for couriers. Within two days the Germans lost approximately seven hundred dead and wounded, and have therefore given up on [open] warfare in favor of destruction by fire. They set fires all over the Ghetto, dropping incendiary bombs from planes, taking care only not to damage Ghetto walls.

> "Nowy Dzien"
> No. 551, April 28, 1943
> *Trans. from Polish*

55. WARSAW, MAY 11, 1943

Report on New Fighting by Bunker Groups in the Ghetto

Ghetto liquidation continues; the last buildings are being burned down. Lately [the Germans] have hit upon several cellars where Jews were hiding. The latter staged a resistance and a battle broke out in which the Germans used anti-tank artillery.

A special commission has arrived from Cracow to investigate the source of the Jews' weapons.

> Ar. of Inst. for Party Hist.
> Sec. III, Delegation Files
> I.M. Report 156
> *Trans. from Polish*

56. WARSAW, MAY 21, 1943

Latest SOS Appeal for Relief from Abroad

To Zygelboim and Szwarczbard:

The heroic struggle in the Warsaw Ghetto still has meaning for the resistance, e.g., the utter dedication and heroism of the Jewish Fighting Organization. Klepfisz, a member of the Bund and pillar of the resistance, died a heroic death. German cruelty is horrid: Jews burned alive, thousands shot or deported to camps, the presidium [1] executed—Lichtenboim, Wielikowski, Sztolcman, and Stanislaw Szereszewski. Several thousand Jews still remain in the Ghetto, underground, and in the shops. The shops, and especially the bunkers, are being liquidated as they stage active and passive resistance.

The Germans systematically set fire to residential blocks, blow them up with mines, or bombard them. The Ghetto, including the sewer exits, has been surrounded by gendarmes. Refugees of the Ghetto inferno are snatched up and executed on the spot. The Jewish Fighting Organization, its day of valor drawing to a close, is still active in the Ghetto. Surviving Jewish centers in the province are also near total liquidation. The world of freedom and justice is silent and does nothing! Astounding! This cable is the third in the past two

---

[1] Of the *Judenrat.*

weeks. Cable immediately about what you've accomplished. We await financial aid for the survivors trying to stay alive.

> Berezowski, for the Central Committee of the Jewish Working Masses in Poland
>
> Borowski, for the Jewish National Committee
>
> Ar. of Inst. for Party Hist.
> Delegation Ar., Cable 90
> *Trans. from Polish*

57. WARSAW, MAY 13, 1943

Report on Twenty-four Days of Fighting in the Warsaw Ghetto and on German Use of Poison Gas

Jewish resistance in the Warsaw Ghetto has not yet been totally extinguished. During the week reported on here, the Germans set fire to the north side of Leszno, damaging the Church of the Holy Virgin Mary. Shooting can be heard night after night. According to a reliable report, the Germans used poison gas on May 9 to do away with Jewish fighters concealed in an underground fortress beneath a building. The members of the *Judenrat* presidium, held hostage at Zelazna 103 from the first day of the Ghetto liquidation, have been executed.

As we write these words the Ghetto Uprising has entered its twenty-fourth day.

> Ar. of Inst. for Party Hist.
> Sec. III, "Bulletin Informacyjny" No. 19 (174),
> May 13, 1943
> *Trans. from Polish*

58. WARSAW, MAY 14, 1943

A Polish Underground Democratic Newspaper on the Appeal of Gov. Fischer [1]

HYPOCRITICAL APPEAL OF GOV. FISCHER

An appeal by Gov. Fischer appeared on Warsaw streets today and expresses the German regime's typical attempt to win over the Polish population for German aims. In so doing, it categorizes the determined fight put up by the Polish underground as an anti-government Communist effort. At the same time, the destruction of the Jewish community is depicted as an act of justice toward . . . Polish citizens, and as revenge for the murder of Polish officers in Katyn. Thus, according to Gov. Fischer, the Ghetto was a Communist nest. At the end of his statement he appeals to Poles to cooperate in the war against Communists. Hoping to provoke "action," he cites the recent Soviet air raid.

A waste of time and paper, Mr. Fischer!

> "Nowy Dzien"
> No. 564, May 14, 1943
> *Trans. from Polish*

[1] After the Soviet air raid, the night of May 13, the Nazi governor of Warsaw, Dr. Ludwig Fischer (sentenced and hanged in Warsaw after the liberation) appealed to the Polish population by warning them against abetting the "Jewish Bolshevik bandits" and asking cooperation with Germans in seizing and combating Jews and Communists.

59. WARSAW, MAY 16, 1943

Cable from Pawel Finder to Georgy Dimitrov about Fighting in the Warsaw Ghetto

From Poland, to Dimitrov:

The battles on Warsaw Ghetto territory have abated; nevertheless they continue into the fourth week. Yesterday the Germans again threw explosives and incendiary bombs. Fires are rampant. The number of Germans killed has reached over a thousand. Five hundred armed Jews broke out of the Ghetto with our aid and made off to the woods.

> Finder

> Ar. of Inst. for Party Hist.
> Polish Comintern Files
> *Trans. from Russian*

60. WASHINGTON, D.C., JANUARY 25, 1958

Letter from Former Land Army Commander in Warsaw Concerning the Ghetto Uprising

Professor Ber Mark
Warsaw

Most Honorable Professor!

I shall try to answer your letter of December 30, 1957 (#2009). I have written to London for certain items, because I do not remember everything. Since their answer has been long in coming, I shall write about the episode retrospectively as it surfaces in my memory.

1. Resistance in the Ghetto was organized by the Jewish Fight-

ing Organization with our modest material assistance, and fullest
—according to prevailing conditions—sharing of tactical knowledge.
We worked through "Antek," who used to meet our diplomatic
officer, "the surgeon" (Stanislaw Weber) chief of area staff, who
provided him, unknown to me, with a number of meeting places. He
also faithfully transmitted all my instructions about battle preparations. We were not informed about the precise moment the battle
was to be launched.

2.   After the fighting began in the Ghetto, all my correspondence
passed through "Waclaw." I would sign brief letters with the
pseudonym, "Konar." The last letter stated that April 23 would be
the day of our greatest battle participation.

3.   From the first day on, we took no part in the fighting. The
same day, a meeting took place (at 12 Marszalkowska Street) where
"Bor," [1] representing "Grot" in the latter's absence, asked me
somewhat boldly whether or not we would help the Jewish Fighting
Organization. Also present were "Grzegorz" (Pelczynski) and "Gil"
(Fildorf). I answered I was ready to take action the very next day,
because everything was ready. We would use diversionary divisions
of the (Warsaw) area led by "Chuchro," [2] a sapper officer. At the
meeting with Bor, I informed those present about plans for a diversionary action for the Ghetto, and this made a strong impression on
them, because they were more ready for a refusal than for our
involvement in the struggle.

4.   Our plan was simple: dynamite the Ghetto walls in order to
facilitate escape for those able and willing. Several holes would be
blasted in the wall near Powonzek and Stawki to enable movement
toward Kampinos Forest. In order to divert the Germans, we would
attack along the entire length of the walls surrounding the Ghetto.
Those who could not go through that way but wanted to escape
would be taken through the sewers.[3]

5.   The action lasted the whole week before Easter due to the
energy displayed by groups (each the size of a platoon) from the
Franciszkanska and Stawki side of the cemetery. I visited one of

---

[1] Gen. Tadeusz Komarowski of the reactionary, anti-Semitic camp.
[2] Jerzy Lewinski, leader of the diversionary section of the A.K. staff.
[3] Nothing ever came of this plan.

these sectors every day, and those involved there knew of my presence.

6. I cannot estimate to what extent our help enabled Rakower's group (three hundred persons [4]) to break through.

7. I shall not say anything about resettling escapees in safe places. This work consumed most of our time. There is no point in going over the details; in any case the efforts helped little.

8. I cannot remember any more the surnames of either squad commanders or soldiers.

9. The Land Army press did not mention these actions for quite understandable reasons. Both the population and the Germans were aware who was capable of carrying out such feats [5] and it was thus superfluous to make the information public. Also, there were some segments of society, fortunately not too many, who were not enthusiastic about helping the Jews or were outright hostile.[6]

10. Weapons were provided well before the Uprising. After that the Jewish Fighting Organization got weapons through its own efforts and quite successfully at that. The Warsaw A.K. had no arsenal of its own in Ghetto territory. Only the A.K. commander-in-chief would have that.

Respectfully,
Gen. Antony Chruszczel ("Monter")

Trans. from Polish

61. WARSAW, MAY 28, 1943

Report of New Clashes in the Nowolipki Square Area

Fighting in the Ghetto goes on. Despite the six-week bombardment with all sorts of weapons, despite the razing by fire of the entire [Jewish] section, despite the use of gas, [the Germans] have not yet

---

[4] Quite an exaggeration.
[5] Self-praise.
[6] I.e., A.K. leadership gave in to anti-Semitic sentiments.

succeeded in breaking the hard core of [Jewish] fighters. At certain spots, including the Nowolipki area, clashes flare up anew. In recent days a cannonade of artillery and machine guns has been heard.

> Ar. of Inst. for Party Hist.
> Sec. III, "Glos Warszawy"
> No. 28 (39), May 28, 1943
> *Trans. from Polish*

62. WARSAW, JUNE 4, 1943

Report on New Clashes in the Warsaw Ghetto, May 31, and June 1, 1943

SELF-DEFENSE CONTINUES IN THE GHETTO

Defense of the Ghetto, which was petering out, has been revived. Figures of fighters have appeared from behind the ruins and, on May 31 and June 1, attacked [German] positions beyond the Ghetto walls. [The Germans] once more brought in fresh reinforcements, mainly Ukrainians—the Germans do not like to die.

> Ar. of Inst. for Party Hist.
> Sec. III, "Glos Warszawy"
> No. 30 (39), June 14, 1943
> *Trans. from Polish*

63. WARSAW, JUNE 10, 1943

Report on Continuation of the Fighting in the Warsaw Ghetto, June 1943

Since April 18, the Warsaw Ghetto has been an arena for armed warfare between Jewish combat groups and German forces. The Germans began the fighting as a reprisal for the Jews' refusal to stop working and show up for deportation. They tried breaking Jewish resistance by dispatching an SS motorcycle detachment to patrol the area and kill anyone they saw. Soon, however, the SS men were pelted with bullets and grenades from Jewish battle squads. They were forced to pull back from the Jewish district, with dead and wounded. Then they brought in well-armed police detachments under cover of tanks, and a battle broke out lasting several hours. The Germans once more were defeated and forced to pull back with casualties. Since then, the fighting has gone on uninterrupted. . . . The Germans began setting fire to entire blocks, and thus far have razed all buildings on Swientojerska, Karmelicka, Franciszkanska, Mila, Muranowska, and Zamenhofa. In addition, they have cut off the flow of water, gas, and electricity to the Ghetto and begun bombarding the area with incendiary bombs and small demolition bombs.

Despite these measures, the Germans can boast thus far of no important military achievement in the Ghetto, and the battle goes on. Jewish combat detachments possess a significant number of weapons (revolvers, light and heavy machine guns, and grenades) and large stores of ammunition and explosive material. The campaign commander is a Polish military officer.[1]

> Ar. of Inst. for Party Hist.
> Sec. III, "Wschod" (the East)
> No. 5 (8), June 10, 1943
> *Trans. from Polish*

---

[1] Perhaps David Apelboim, Farband commander and lieutenant in the Polish Army.

64. WARSAW, JUNE 21, 1943

Notification Abroad about Continuing the Struggle in the Forest

Some of the fighters broke through to the forest and continue to struggle. Among them is one of our detachments headed by Berlinski.[1]

The provincial ghettoes intend to, and will, defend themselves.

> Adolf [2] and Antony [3]
>
> Ar. of Inst. for Party Hist.
> Sec. III, Delegation Files
> Cable 111b
> *Trans. from Polish*

65. WARSAW, JULY 1943

Report on the Last Phase of the Ghetto Uprising, from a German Citation Recommendation for Schupo Maj. Otto Bundke

Maj. Bundke, as commander of the 3rd SS and 23rd Police,[1] took part in the final pacification action in the former Jewish residential district, and through his own acts and outstanding leadership ability, was able to produce tangible achievements.

---

[1] Referred to here are the two Fighting Organization squads that escaped through the sewers and continued on to Wyszkow Forest. There they formed a partisan contingent under Adam Szwarcfus, Mordekhai Growas, Ignac, and others. Berlinski was there too, and later returned to Warsaw.

[2] Berman.

[3] Nathan Buksboim, Left Labor Zionist activist, who perished later in Auschwitz.

---

[1] Police Battalion.

After the pullback [2] of *Waffen SS* troops the battalion was forced to carry out all assignments alone. The enemy [the Jewish fighters] having become aware of the diminution of [our] forces, sent their gangs to attack once more. With this intensified fighting by the well-armed, well-led bands, it became necessary to combat resistance nests concealed among ruins, cellars, and underground channels.

Maj. Bundke's accomplishment consisted in effectively absorbing compiled intelligence material in leading the liquidation action against remaining bands. During a number of assaults Bundke himself assumed command, serving his soldiers as a model of daring. He was in the midst of fire in every battle. After the final liquidation of the nests of rebellion, he took upon himself the responsibility for security in the former Jewish residential district and was deployed in a series of major actions in metropolitan Warsaw. He has also performed notable accomplishments in recent months in carrying out special assignments [executions] . . .

> Ar. of High Commission to Investigate Nazi War
>   Crimes in Poland
> Citation Proposals
> *Trans. from German*

66. WARSAW, JULY 1943

Report on Battles in the Warsaw Ghetto in June and July 1943, from a German Citation Recommendation for Schupo *Capt. Ederer*

During the campaign in the former Jewish residential district of Warsaw, in July 1943, Capt. Ederer personally participated in an armed struggle with nine armed Jewish [outlaws] and caused these armed Jews to be rendered harmless.

In June 1943, while battling and overwhelming a bandit's nest in

---

[2] May 16, when Stroop declared the campaign officially over.

the former Jewish residential district in Warsaw, Ederer distinguished himself in combating the Jewish–Bolshevik outlaws.

> Ar. of High Commission to Investigate Nazi War
> Crimes in Poland
> Citation Proposals
> *Trans. from German*

67. WARSAW, MAY 8, 1943

A.K. Commander-in-Chief Gen. Rowecki's Report to London on the Progress of the Uprising in the Warsaw Ghetto

On April 19, SS detachments, plus formations of Lithuanians, Latvians, and Ukrainians, entered the Warsaw Ghetto with the objective of wiping it out. They were attacked by the Jewish Fighting Organization groups stationed at preassigned battle stations that would be held by the latter until April 23. The Germans also introduced planes and tanks; one of the latter was burned [by the Jews]. From the 23rd through the 28th, the insurrection continued in the form of partisan street fighting, especially at night. Subsequently, the [Jewish] fighters staged resistance from barricaded buildings for a few days, but that resistance, too, has been broken.

The Germans' main weapon has been systematic setting of fires that still burn in the Ghetto. Through April 30, [the Germans] led fourteen thousand Jews to their doom—three thousand by burning, two thousand executed on the spot. These numbers climb along with the liquidation of the hiding places.

An account of the armed support we provided the Jews will be given in a special memorandum to the "h.c." staff.[1]

The liquidation of the Warsaw Ghetto, which began April 19, of this year, is just about complete. It follows an incredibly strong Jewish Uprising that aroused confusion among the Germans and

---

[1] We have not found this memorandum. That it was designated exclusively for the commander-in-chief in London demonstrates again the A.K. leadership's tendency to cover up the "Chwatski" group's action on Sapiezynska.

forced the latter to introduce into the action numerous detachments of gendarmes and SS, plus Ukrainian and Latvian auxiliary formations, and to use tanks, artillery, flame throwers, and even incendiary bombs dropped from planes. After the first week of fighting, the Germans were forced by their numerous casualties to change tactics. They then began razing entire residential areas; cutting off electricity, gas, and water; and blocking the sewers through which the [Jewish] fighters maintained contact with the rest of the city. At the time, all Warsaw was engulfed by clouds of pungent smoke, illuminated at night by the flames and shaken by reverberations from the explosions. Normal communication with Zoliborz and Powonzek was completely cut off, but has been continued since along the banks of the Vistula by horse and wagon.

Although in recent days the Uprising has virtually ceased, the [Germans] continue to burn alive anyone who has preferred to hide within the well-developed bunker system rather than surrender.

The Germans fire at anyone trying to save himself, and forbid fire fighters to quench the human torches. A Danteesque scenario has been enacted in the Ghetto, transcending anything that happened there before.

It is worth mentioning that burning the Ghetto also brought disruption and loss to nearby Aryan sections of the city. Among places damaged were a significant portion of Leszno Street, including the Church of the Holy Virgin Mary, and a series of historical buildings and residences. The Evangelist Hospital, endangered by the fires, had to evacuate within twenty-four hours under horrid conditions.

As I write this report (May 7, of this year), resistance activity appears to have ceased except for isolated acts of defense by some fighters hiding in the ruins. There is also an occasional explosion in a munitions warehouse resulting from contact with flames from the still-active conflagration.[2]

All Jews who presented themselves for deportation were then taken toward Lublin. Many jumped from the train and crippled themselves, or perished from the fall or their escorts' machine gun bullets. For those who got away, search expeditions are being sent.

---

[2] Later there were also major clashes in the Ghetto.

During the Uprising, a number of Jews succeeded in getting across Ghetto walls and hiding in the city, but [the Germans] conduct expeditions and house-to-house searches to capture these fugitives. This causes much misunderstanding and frequent extorting of money.

Kalina

C.Ar. of I.M., A.K. Ar.
Survey of Critical Events of April 24–May 7, 1943

The battles of the Jewish Fighting Organization in the Warsaw Ghetto go into their tenth week. In the action, the Germans deploy in addition to SS and gendarmes: Lithuanian and Turkoman [3] detachments, artillery, tanks, planes (incendiary bombs), and flame throwers.

The Jewish fighters rejected the German ultimatum to surrender, and continue defending themselves. In the past few weeks [the Germans] have begun definitive extermination action either through on-the-spot execution or deportation to Auschwitz and the Cracow or Stanislaw Ghetto.

Kalina

C.Ar. of I.M., A.K. Ar.
Cable 733, May 10, 1943

Jewish Affairs: The "cleanup" of Ghetto territory goes on. Buildings are demolished or burned under the pretext that refugees are hiding there and doing underground work. [The Germans] have even burned houses on the Aryan side, giving the proprietors two hours for evacuation.

During the "cleanup" the Germans occasionally clash with Jewish combat squads hiding in holes or nooks underground. When uncovered, the fighters offer individual resistance.

The Germans consider the prolonged resistance a disgrace.

---

[3] The Turkomans were Moslems serving in the Soviet Army, from which they were captured and then recruited for "national" detachments.

Warsaw Higher SS and Police Chief von Sammern has been blamed for allowing it to form in the first place, and has been dismissed; Police Gen. Stroop has taken his place.

C.Ar. of I.M., A.K. Ar.
Survey of Critical Events in Poland
May 8, 1943
Trans. from Polish

68. WARSAW, JULY 28, 1943

Letter from a Native German Woman from Warsaw to the SS Command, Concerning the Uprising in the Ghetto and Overall Conditions in Warsaw

Personal Staff of *SS Reichsfuehrer.* 343

REPORT ON WARSAW

(Transmitted by SS Col. von Karzawski.) Experiences and conclusions of a native German woman who spent eight months in Warsaw.

THE GENERAL SITUATION

Dating from first counterattacks on the eastern front, begun December 1942,[1] great insecurity has reigned in Warsaw. Every day there are attacks on soldiers of the *Wehrmacht* [shootings] and on officials of civilian institutions. Two agencies received bombs in mail parcels. In addition there have been many threatening letters, an attack on a bank, and assassinations carried out in a government printing house. The last-mentioned occurred on March 3, when the two German directors of the printing house were shot after the watchmen were disarmed. Three men lured the officials out of their

---

[1] Refers to the Soviet counter-offensive at Stalingrad.

apartment into the street. One wore the uniform of a gendarme, the second was dressed as a member of the SD, and the third was in civilian clothes and spoke fluent German. After searching without success for the keys to the safe in the printing house, they shot [the German executives] in the neck in the watchman's room. Also assassinated was the labor bureau chief, during work hours in his office. His assistant was shot in the street.

On March 16, an SA detachment—returning from the memorial service of music for the third in charge of the labor bureau—was assaulted by grenades and fifteen persons were wounded.

Plans for the SS action to be carried out the next day, and prepared in great secrecy, were uncovered. When the SS entered the Ghetto in trucks it was fired upon from all sides. Liquidating the Ghetto, instead of lasting an estimated three to four days, went on for five weeks. Under Ghetto buildings there is an impenetrable maze of passages, connecting a well-disguised bunker network and leading through sewer exits as far as the Vistula in the Polish sector. A wealth of property has been destroyed, and Jews and gangs continue attacking, even after termination of the Ghetto campaign. Grenades were thrown at the Adriatic Lounge and a coffee shop in the central railroad station. The Warsaw economy has been hit by recent attacks on dairy firms.

> Ar. of High Commission to Investigate Nazi War
>   Crimes in Poland
> Minutes of the Biller Trial, vol. XI from Doc. Center
>   702
> *Trans. from German*

69. WARSAW, DECEMBER 22, 1943

Report about Uncovering an Armed Jewish Group

The Gestapo discovered a group of sixty-two Jews in the cellar of a building on Krolewska Street. They had large supplies of food and weapons. All were murdered.

> Ar. of Inst. for Party Hist.
> Delegation Files
> Dept. of the Interior, Report No. 238
> *Trans. from Polish*

70. WARSAW, JULY 7, 1944

Report of a Clash Involving a Jewish Group Among Ghetto Ruins in June 1944

For over a year, Jewish groups have holed up in bunkers under cellars of burned-out buildings. They are killed on the spot. In the middle of June 1944, a bunker with three Jews inside was discovered; they resisted and killed three Germans. The latter killed twenty-five Jews in retaliation. The three Jews were then incorporated into groups of foreign Jews. Workers demolishing the ruins of [burned out] houses often find weapons, money, and valuable objects there.

> "Informacja Narodowa i Wschodnia"
> (National and Eastern Reports)
> July 7, 1944
> *Trans. from Polish*

71. WARSAW, MARCH 13, 1944

Notification on Uncovering the Bunker of Emmanuel Ringelblum

A bunker with Jews was discovered on Grojecka 81 near Wolski's.[1]

Ar. of Inst. for Party Hist.
Delegation Materials
Intelligence Files, Report No. 281
Trans. from Polish

72. WARSAW, MAY 1, 1944

Evaluation of the Ghetto Uprising in the Central Publication of the P.P.R.

A full-fledged battle flared up in the center of Warsaw on April 19, 1943. The Jews, incarcerated behind Ghetto walls, had decided to defend themselves rather than be sent to the new Poniatow and Trawniki death camps. The brown murderers who intended to force the Jews into the wagons were greeted by machine-gun and pistol fire. The SS and police chief expected that with the help of his armor he would crush the Jewish resistance within hours. Tanks moved into Ghetto streets, followed by infantry. Instead of anti-tank artillery the Jews used grenades and bottles of benzine, and with this primitive defense repulsed the initial German frontal assault.

During the first two days, the Germans often tried to seize the Jewish positions, but each time the fighters held their ground. Ger-

---

[1] There was a bunker on Grojecka 81 where some thirty-three Jews were concealed, among them Ringelblum, his wife, and his only son. Mieczyslaw Wolski was one of the Poles who set up and guarded the bunker. All Jews there, and Wolski, were shot.

man casualties reached almost two hundred dead and wounded. Frontal assault on the Ghetto proved fruitless; each building had been transformed into a fortress. The network of underground passages enabled unexpected assaults upon the enemy.

Subsequently, the Germans began a siege of the Ghetto. They introduced artillery and systematically bombarded building after building. At the same time, airplanes saturated the battle sector with incendiary bombs and for three weeks the flames raged, devouring a quarter of the city.

Ghetto defense was led by a young fighter by the name of Anielewicz, who acquired his military skill and experience during the battle. With minimal help from outside and poorly endowed with weapons and ammunition, the Jewish Fighting Organization staged a heroic resistance against an opponent stronger by a hundredfold. Although they were brutally beaten, the Ghetto fighters' struggle proved to the world that even under the worst conditions an armed opponent can be smacked in the teeth. The April campaign was lost because the Jews were pitted against the modern Hitler war machine and because moral and political errors were committed in the summer of 1942, when with a determined attack they could still have nullified the plans of Nazi killers.

[. . .] the Jews' armed rebellion was not mere improvisation or an act of desperation; it had been planned for months. After August and September 1942, the Jews no longer had any illusion about the fate prepared for them by the occupation forces. They drew conclusions based upon the tragic events of those days.

The Jewish community reached a consensus among all political factions, and a united democratic front [1] was set up excluding the official communal body [2] and Jewish fascists,[3] open collaborators of the German murderers. Jewish workers formed the core of the resistance front and the Jewish Fighting Organization based itself upon that foundation. Military preparations were undertaken, bunkers were constructed, food and weapon supplies were gathered.

---

[1] The Anti-Fascist Bloc.

[2] The *Judenrat.*

[3] Jewish police, shop managers, etc.

On the first anniversary of the heroic battles in the Warsaw Ghetto, we pay our respects to the Jews who fell in the unforgettable April days in the struggle against the Nazi enemy.

"Tribuna Wolnoszczy" [4]
(Freedom's Tribune)
May 1, 1944
Trans. from Polish

73. WARSAW, MAY 14, 1943

Evaluation of the Ghetto Insurrection in a Polish Underground Democratic Newspaper

Glory to the Vanquished! Saragossa—Alcazar—Stalingrad—Nalewki.

The last pockets of resistance fight without hope. Fires flicker into the night. The sun, setting behind artful clouds, creates special effects. Has no painter yet immortalized the symbol of our day in a panorama—"Smoke over Warsaw?" I approach the front—more accurately, a gigantic cemetery. No natural catastrophe has yet caused so huge a grave.

Stillness of a mass grave. No more joyful announcements over the megaphone: "We've taken the Muranowski front." No short-wave warnings reaching the German staff headquarters: "We can defend ourselves for two weeks!" An era has ended.

Near a freshly demolished house, soldiers take target practice with pistols. Not enough experience yet, despite the firing range they had for themselves? But then, what are their hands for, if not murder? The more helpless the victim, the greater the satisfaction. Breaking into a hospital like the angel of death, approaching a patient and leaving a corpse; snatching an infant from a mother,

---

[4] Chief organ of the P.P.R.

cracking tiny head against tiny head and splattering a wall with brains—that's their specialty. . . .

The defense of Nalewki will enter the annals of history like that of Saragossa, Alcazar, Westerplatte, Stalingrad, and every place where blood had been spilled in defense. Nalewki was doomed from the start—what were they doing, defending the honor of the flag? We followed the struggle with horror and compassion; we observed its stages, our eyes and ears turned to the fire in the heavens.

"Glory to the vanquished!" said Orzeszkowa to the rebels in 1863, revising the Latin, "Woe to the vanquished." The defeated have earned this loving mark of distinction, the heroes of the January struggle and the heroes of the September 1939 campaign. I do not insult our heroes of 1939 by comparing them to the Warsaw martyrs: the vanquished have always been entitled to glory after death, provided they struggled with courage and heroism. The Ghetto defenders were not only defeated by overpowering, brutal soldiers of terror but also put through the worst array of tortures human beings can inflict upon each other. A fresh page has been added to the chronicle of sadistic massacre.

In both a literal and symbolic sense, the defenders left the world as a burnt offering; and with the assurance that civilization will glorify their memories.

"Nowy Dzien"
No. 564, May 14, 1943
Trans. from Polish

74. LONDON

Cable from Abroad Concerning Difficulties in Rescue Work

To the Polish government-in-exile on behalf of the representative of the Jewish National Committee:

Throughout the entire war period we have been looking for

means of communicating with you and providing relief. Unfortunately, we find unmitigated resistance and indifference on the part of those who could possibly rescue you.

> Committee to Rescue Jews in Occupied Europe [1]

> Ar. of Inst. for Party Hist.
> Sec. III, Delegation Files
> Cable from Abroad No. 16
> *Trans. from Polish*

75. WARSAW, OCTOBER 24, 1943

Memorandum of the Jewish Mutiny in Sobibor

During the second half of October, Jews mutinied successfully in the Sobibor death camp. Several hundred camp inmates killed their executioners, scores of SS men, and Ukrainians. After setting fire to the camp all the inmates fled.

> Ar. of Inst. for Party Hist.
> Delegation Files: "Pro Memoria"
> On Internal Conditions
> *Trans. from Polish*

---

[1] Va'ad ha-Hatzala. The cable was sent by Va'ad chairman Itzhak Greenbaum from Palestine.

---

[1] The mutiny broke out October 14, 1943.

76. WARSAW, OCTOBER 25, 1943

Cable Concerning Clashes in the Bialystok Ghetto, Treblinka, and Sobibor in August and October 1943

To Szwarczbard:

We received your cables of September 2, and October 1; the agony of the survivors of Polish Jewry still continues. After the ghastly extermination of the Ghettoes in Bedzin, Vilna, Bialystok, and Torno, there were more massacres in a number of smaller camps. The heroic struggle of the Jews in Bialystok [1] set an example for a number of camps readying for their own resistance. Two such death camps were destroyed and burned after a heroic fight: Treblinka [2] and Sobibor. With relief and rescue activities expanding each passing week, financial aid received thus far is inadequate. In the past four months, we have received just two payments of $10,000 plus £10,000 you sent four months ago. Neither the £9,000 nor £15,000 sum mentioned in your October 4 cable has reached Warsaw, and as yet there has been no official explanation.

See to it the money is sent to us immediately. This is a life-and-death issue for thousands of persons. In a few days it may be too late. In view of their defeat, the Germans are planning a general slaughter of remaining Jews. Doesn't the American Joint [Distribution Committee] exist anymore? Why don't they send money? Pay attention to the camps of Vitel and Bergen [3] near Hanover. Starvation rules apply in Bergen, and contact with the outside is prohibited. Arrange for intervention from the International Red Cross and the

---

[1] Insurrection in the Bialystok Ghetto erupted August 16, 1943.

[2] The revolt in Treblinka took place August 2, 1943.

[3] In concentration camps in Vitel, France and Bergen-Belsen, Germany, there were groups of Jews from Warsaw and other Polish cities.

Swiss Legation in Germany. Do your efforts in Stockholm vis-à-vis the children have any chance of success? Save the children. Warm greetings to everyone.

> Jewish National Committee
> Borowski, Izhak, Tsivia, Caftor [4]

> Ar. of Inst. for Party Hist.
> German Section, Delegation Files
> *Trans. from Polish*

77. WARSAW, OCTOBER 26, 1943

Report on Armed Resistance in the Tarnow Ghetto in September 1943

On September 1–2, 1943, the ghetto in Tarnow was liquidated. The Jews defended themselves during the liquidation. The Germans used grenades to break the resistance. Up to 150 Jews per car were loaded into freight cars, the insides of which were covered with carbide and lime. Then the cars were sealed, inundated with water, and sent off to extermination.

> "Glos Warszawy"
> No. 67 (76), October 26, 1943
> *Trans. from Polish*

78. WARSAW, NOVEMBER 16, 1943

Report on the Jewish Mutiny in Sobibor

The pace of liquidation in the camps has quickened. Inmates are machine gunned. The camps where Jews were interned were first in line. November 3, the Trawniki camp with its three thousand Jews

---

[4] The last three names stand for Itzhak Cukierman, Tsivia Lubetkin, and David Guzik.

was liquidated. Expecting the worst, the Jews had made ready to defend themselves. In order to dull the awareness of these victims before the action, the camp administration earlier had softened conditions by improving food, enlarging workshops, and bringing in a large supply of raw materials. In order to further fool the inmates, [the Germans] ordered the Jews to dig air raid trenches. While the Jews were thus occupied, they were exterminated with machine-gun fire. The same happened to the women later in the day. At the same time, fifteen thousand Jews in the Poniatow camp were also executed.

Meanwhile, the Jews in the Sobibor camp were able to find out about the schemes of the murderers and disarmed camp personnel—SS men and Ukrainians. They then set fire to the barracks and made off to the woods. About five hundred persons were saved.

"Glos Warszawy"
No. 73 (82), November 16, 1943
Trans. from Polish

79. WARSAW, DECEMBER 10, 1943

Report on the Mutiny of Jewish Inmates of Treblinka in August 1943

NEWS FROM TREBLINKA: In the past week, news has reached Warsaw about events in the infamous death factory, the Treblinka camp. Based on fragmentary reports, here is an account of events there.

Three thousand Jews had been kept in the camp to bury the bodies of the thousands of murdered victims and were forced, at gunpoint, to tend gas chambers, and so on. These unfortunate victims, who occasionally after being "used" would themselves be done away with, finally mutinied. Driven by despair and confusion, the Jews did away with scores of Gestapo personnel, took over the arsenal, armed themselves, burned down part of the camp, then escaped to the surrounding woods. Approximately two thousand eight hundred persons, most of them armed, made it to the forest. There they engaged in partisan warfare and delivered some painful blows to the search expeditions sent after them.

> "Glos Warszawy"
> No. 49 (58), December 10, 1943
> *Trans. from Polish*

80. WARSAW, OCTOBER–DECEMBER 1943

Notification to the Nation about the Jewish Uprising in Lvov Ghetto and in the Poniatow Camp

Jews, the few remaining Jews in Lvov have been murdered after offering active resistance. Ten thousand were killed in the Trawniki camp. During the massacre of fifteen thousand in Poniatow, one barracks staged an armed resistance, and was destroyed by burning. A massacre of Jews took place in Majdanek on November 5; only five thousand are still detained in the castle. Altogether, forty thousand Jews were killed in the Lublin district in the first ten days of November.

On October 14, six hundred Jews escaped from the Sobibor torture camp after doing away with the German guard.

Five hundred are deported daily from the Lodz Ghetto. By the end of November, only one hundred fifty thousand Jews, half of whom are foreigners, [remained] in "legal" settlements in Poland.

> Ar. of I.M., A.K. Ar.
> "Bulletin from the Bases"
> *Trans. from Polish*

81. WARSAW, NOVEMBER 23, 1943

SOS to the Bund Central Committee in New York

You certainly must receive information from and about us from London. Now the remnants of Polish Jewry are being wiped out. The situation is tragic. Let the world know. Responsibility to posterity for murder of the innocent also falls upon the democracies. Why don't you maintain contact with us?

Berezowski, for the Central Committee of the Bund

Ar. of Inst. for Party Hist.
Delegation Files, Cable 201
Trans. from Polish

82. DECEMBER 1964

Survey of the Activity of the Department of Jewish Affairs of the A.K. High Command

1. This department was formed November 11, 1942. Its task at first was limited to information gathering. It drew upon a series of private contacts in the Warsaw Ghetto, and upon private individuals arriving daily from the provinces, especially from Soviet-held Ukraine. The Warsaw Ghetto also was the source of detailed and reliable information on the condition of Jews in the provinces. The department's own intelligence network at this time provided little reliable [information] on the Jews. Its typical contacts were Polish intellectuals of Jewish origin with official positions in Ghetto institutions (the council, hospitals, or the Bund). Contact with Jewish nationalist circles was as yet indirect.

Aside from the ongoing information service, which also functioned throughout the [July–September 1942] Warsaw Ghetto liquidation, the department prepared an overall report on the condition of the Jews in Poland. When the first "Black Book" reached headquarters [1] in early December 1942, we published it immediately after minor editing.

2. The initiative to create the Council to Aid Jews came the end of August [1942] from our inner circles, and the project was subsequently taken over by the Delegation and communal-political groups. Thanks to this initiative ZEGOTA[2] was set up as a government-in-exile department [early fall, 1942], and in December 1942, the first relief stipends were issued by this department.

3. The first official contact between the Warsaw Ghetto and the military [3] was established near the end of the liquidation there [late August 1942]. Mikolaj, the Bund representative, set up the contact with the department and requested a cable be sent to Zygelboim, Jewish National Council member at central headquarters. The cable, depicting the situation in a few words, asked for financial aid and was dispatched. In October [1942], Mikolaj received $5,000.

4. In December 1942, thanks to the intercession of the head [4] of our "Harcerz" bureau, representatives of Jewish pioneering youth movements got through to the department. Contact was made with Jurek [5] as representative of the Jewish National Committee, which is comprised of all political factions in the Jewish community except the Bund. The Jewish National Committee collaborated with the Bund, which preferred political isolation to joining the Committee. The structure that united the two bodies was called the Coordinating Commission and served as the political arm of the Jewish Fighting Organization.

During the first meeting, Jurek declared that this was his second attempt to set up contact with the military in Poland. The first was in August [1942], during the intensive liquidation of the Ghetto; the goal then was to obtain help in organizing armed resistance against

---

[1] In London.
[2] Jewish affairs bureau.
[3] A.K.
[4] Prof. Alexander Kaminski, also editor of "Bulletin Informacyjny."
[5] Aryeh Wilner.

the German faction, but the response from the military authorities was negative. On my recommendation the [A.K.] high command launched an investigation of the matter that confirmed both Jurek's claim and the private nature of the rejection.

Jurek then requested that contact be established between representatives of the Jewish community and the Polish military and civilian authorities in the country, in order to coordinate their efforts and also to secure aid from the military for the Jewish Fighting Organization. Two such similar requests from the Coordinating Commission signed by Jurek and Mikolaj were then sent to the A.K. commander-in-chief and the Polish government-in-exile. In a statement issued November 11, 1942, the commander-in-chief agreed to take the matter under advisement, and praised the battle readiness of the Fighting Organization, authorizing it to organize in units of five. The Government response was imparted orally.

I personally informed Jurek and Mikolaj about the recognition of their request after being authorized to do so by Thomas [6] and Grochowiecki [7] in late November 1942. Thus began contacts and cooperation between the A.K. military high command and the Delegation on one side, and representatives of the Jewish population on the other.

4. About the time the contacts were set up, the department, in addition to the information work, was also concerned with general contact and cooperation with Jewish organizations. In the military area, Jewish activists were eager to procure weapons and training in preparation for the final battle in the Ghetto. The Jewish Fighting Organization held tenaciously to the belief that the Ghetto was doomed, and sooner or later, like all other Jewish communities, would be wiped out; it is, therefore, better to die with honor, with weapons in hand. In December 1942, after urgent pleading, the [A.K.] commander-in-chief ordered the Jewish Fighting Organization be given ten pistols and a small amount of ammunition. The arms were in poor condition and not fully functional. The Fighting Organization viewed the gift as meeting only a partial need and

---

[6] Thomas Makowiecki, a Jew and member of the A.K. propaganda department.
[7] Delegation representative.

requested much additional help, expressing readiness to pay the necessary price with funds designated by central headquarters for the purpose. The demand was attended to minimally—for January 17, 1943, (projected liquidation date for fifty thousand Warsaw Ghetto inmates) the Fighting Organization received ten additional pistols, instruction in diversionary action and military demeanor, and directions for preparing Molotov cocktails.

In anticipation of January 17, the Jewish Fighting Organization engaged in feverish battle preparations, continually pressuring the military authority with demands to which the latter reacted with disbelief and reserve. The Ghetto liquidation, begun January 17, encountered a determined armed resistance, that undoubtedly aroused the German murderers' consternation, and brought about a halt to the action after four days. Evaluating its victory, the Jewish Fighting Organization concluded that it was temporary and that extinction was merely postponed a while; with renewed energy they continued preparing for the next round, and more insistently demanded aid from the military. In accordance with the order of the A.K. commander-in-chief, I discussed the matter with "Drapacz" [8] commander Mr. Konar.[9] He agreed to provide the Ghetto with both materiel and instruction, and proceeded to check the possibility of getting aid from our detachments abroad. Work began immediately under "the surgeon." [10]

Contact was set up between Jurek, of the Fighting Organization, and our officers. We gave the Fighting Organization about fifty pistols, much ammunition, about 80 kilograms of incendiary material, and a number of defensive grenades. A Molotov cocktail factory was formed in the Ghetto. We also aided in the arms purchase the Fighting Organization was engaged in. Together, we worked out a plan for Ghetto fighting, in which help from our detachments was anticipated.

Our cooperative efforts were disrupted when Jurek was arrested March 6, 1943 (in a Wspolna Street apartment). Soon after, I had a conversation with Konar about finalizing the degree to which we

[8] Name for Warsaw A.K.
[9] Antony Chruszczel ("Monter").
[10] Weber, a Pole, chief of Warsaw A.K. office.

would commit our troops in the embattled Ghetto. We saw our task as leading out possibly great numbers of Jews from Warsaw and resettling them in places I could mention if requested. This project was never realized; not one detachment moved into its assigned area. The Jewish Fighting Organization considered it impossible to tear away some of its forces to areas hundreds of kilometers away, and resettlement in "Len" [11] or "Hreczko" [12] afforded inadequate relief.

Accepting Jews into our military divisions in the "Drapacz" and "Cegielnia" [13] sectors had been judged impossible; on the other hand, Konar gave his approval to the creation of passive-resistance details among the Jews, and such a body was created in Warsaw with one of our officers in charge of training. At the training spot, the latter arranged a further meeting but never returned. After much effort, the officer came to the site once more, but was dead drunk. Further efforts proved fruitless. The Jewish resistance detail received no training and ceased to exist.

5. Cooperation between the military authority and Jewish organizations was not to be limited to Warsaw and was to have embraced all Poland. In February 1943, the [A.K.] commander-in-chief ordered weapons delivered to the sealed ghettoes that wished to defend themselves.[14] According to that order, Polish military [A.K.] commands were to give all possible assistance to Jewish communities subordinate to the Fighting Organization and the Coordinating Commission. Implementation of this order—which the Jewish organizations and those who wanted to wage war in the Ghetto had been urging so strongly—aroused opposition from local military elements. The order was essentially carried out—after intercession by the high command—only in the Bialystok Ghetto, which, according to "the surgeon's" information, received substantial military assistance (a vehicle, weapons, etc.).[15]

---

[11] Name for A.K.-designated sector in Lublin.
[12] Name for A.K.-designated sector in Wolyn.
[13] A.K.-designated sector at the edge of Warsaw.
[14] This order was sabotaged by the majority of the A.K. leadership in the province.
[15] This has not been confirmed by Jewish underground sources from the Bialystok Ghetto.

As a result of the February 1943 order, a contact was set up with Jewish labor circles in Czestochowa and preparations began for what turned out to be an unsuccessful self-defense in the Poniatow and Trawniki camps. The unfriendly reception there, contrary to the spirit of the order, was the work of our details who opposed the Jewish Fighting Organization detachment hiding in the Koniecpol area and asking to be accepted by us. The Fighting Organization detail was massacred twice by an "Orzel" group (probably the N.S.Z.),[16] despite our instructions to the local command to aid the detachment.

6. In addition to the above, the military came to the assistance of the Jewish Fighting Organization in yet another way—facilitating communications abroad, by sending many cables to representatives of the Jews on the National Council, and also to Jewish bodies in England, America, and Palestine. The Fighting Organization also benefited from legal assistance, such as receiving document forms, instructions on filling them out and sealing them. Security measures were also provided by us. Antek and Borowski were able to move about because we pursued and killed German agents who were in pursuit of the Fighting Organization personnel, and posed a constant menace to that body.

7. The department served central headquarters in gathering information and disseminating propaganda. Besides the aforementioned first "Black Book," two large collections of information and documents concerning the liquidation of Jews in Warsaw and Poland at large were sent to London and published in English as the second "Black Book." Also, as part of its regular function, the department provided the commander-in-chief and bases in Poland with information (both periodicals and special dispatches).

8. During the entire life of the department (until August 1, 1944) there was a real appreciation, coming out of political considerations, of the need for an improved relationship with the Jews; there was much mistrust on the part of the latter, and this was felt

---

[16] Extreme reactionaries, an openly anti-Semitic military contingent in the Polish underground.

quite keenly by Jewish representatives with whom I came into contact. They told me more than once that Konar's officers, in working with Jurek, whom they held in high regard, spontaneously expressed in his absence their mistrust and ill will toward the Jews. During an effective—at least from a propaganda standpoint—conveyance of weapons into the Ghetto, performed by our people and led by Jurek, negative sentiments were expressed toward the Jews. This despite the precise, bold execution of the mission. Jurek strongly sensed this hostility.

Other negative gestures to the Jews included a second instructor leaving his post within the Jewish Fighting Organization, and also the refusal to accept into our ranks a Jewish detachment at the time of the Uprising. The latter waited pointlessly for twenty-four hours to be received by an A.K. officer. Finally, Antek,[17] the Fighting Organization commander, was informed that it would be impossible for a Jewish detail to join the A.K. (This information stems from Jewish sources, and I have not confirmed it with Poles.)

9. At this point, Jewish matters hold much political significance for us—especially when the peace conference will take place, and for this reason we must keep working with them. After their experiences during the Uprising, the Jews display no initiative toward joint struggle with the A.K. against the Germans. Efforts in this direction have come up against a crisis in belief.

There exists now, to my knowledge, one Jewish community, in Czestochowa (in the concentration camp [18]) of ten thousand persons, which limits the scope of cooperative action.

It still makes sense for us to stress and document our concern for the fate of Jewish citizens during the final period of the war, by establishing contact with the Czestochowa community. Joint work should be facilitated there through a contact made by order of the commander-in-chief, shortly before the Uprising (by "Rosmaryn" of "Rolnik" [19]) broke out there. An investigation, through our con-

[17] Itzhak Cukierman.
[18] Hasag.
[19] Couriers of the Jewish Fighting Organization working with the Jewish underground in "Hasag" were Maria Waniewicza and Faygl Peltel-Miedzyrzecka.

tact, of events there and how we could provide assistance would be the final document we could compile testifying to our cooperation with the Jewish community in military affairs.

Zakszewski [20]

C.A.r. of I.M.
Delegation File 458
Trans. from Polish

83. WARSAW, APRIL 19, 1944

Cable from the Jewish Workers Alliance [1] to Moscow, c/o The Union of Polish Patriots and the Jewish Anti-Fascist Committee

The Jewish Workers Alliance requests publication of the following cable in the Soviet press.

To the Union of Polish patriots and the Jewish anti-Fascist Committee in Moscow:

In connection with the anniversary of the heroic struggle in the Warsaw Ghetto, we send battle greetings to the victorious Soviet Army, to Gen. Berling's Polish Army, and to Jewish workers throughout the world, battling for economic and national liberation. The handful of Polish Jews still in torture camps, those hiding in cities and forests, those cruelly wiped out by the Hitlerite murderers and their henchmen, place all their hopes upon a victorious Red Army. Jewish workers fight under the slogan of the national council: "For Freedom, Democracy and a Peoples Poland."

Jewish Workers Alliance in Poland
Ar. of Central Comm. of P.P.R.
Document Collection of the National Council, Sec. 2,
   No. 27
Trans. from Russian

---

[20] Henryk Wolynski (Waclaw).

[1] Name of a group of Left Labor Zionist and Communist activists who joined the National Council.

84. WARSAW, APRIL 19, 1945

Order of the High Command of the Polish Army Concerning Awards Posthumously Accorded the Most Meritorious Fighters of the Ghetto Uprising

On the basis of a decree of the Polish Committee of National Liberation, dated December 23, 1944, and on behalf of the President of the National Land Council—on the occasion of the second anniversary of the Warsaw Ghetto Uprising—I hereby confer posthumously the following decorations to the meritorious participants of that revolt:

GRUNWALD CROSS, CLASS III

Anielewicz, Mordekhai
Kartin, Pinya (Andrejz Schmidt)
Lewartowski, Joseph
Platnycka, Frume [1]
Kaplan, Joseph
Tenenboim, Mordekhai (Tamarov) [2]
Teitelboim, Nuita (Wanda)

CROSS VIRTUTI MILITARI, CLASS V

Zagan, Shakhne
Blum, Abrasza
Wittenberg, Itzak [3]
Lejbowicz, Laban [4]

[1] Representative of the Jewish National Committee and the Jewish Fighting Organization in the Bedzin Ghetto. He perished there during armed self-defense.

[2] Representative of the Jewish National Committee and the Jewish Fighting Organization in the Bialystok Ghetto. He was killed during the Uprising of August 1943.

[3] Commander of the United Organization of Partisans of the Vilna Ghetto; murdered by the Gestapo.

[4] Member of the Jewish Fighting Organization of the Cracow Ghetto; murdered by the Gestapo.

Kaganowicz [5]
Jeger, Samuel [6]
Chojnik, Abram [7]
Roisenfeld, Michal
Berlinski, Hersz
Fondaminski, Ephraim
Cymerman, Meretyk
Wilner, Aryeh (Jurek)
Breslaw, Szmul

CROSS OF THE BRAVE

Dr. Chorozycki [8]
Glanc, Rywka [9]
Kot, Abram
Szeingut, Tuvia (Tadek) [10]
Gott, Leyb [11]
Gutman, Henoch
Farber, Joseph
Artszteyn, Zekhariah
Fiszlewicz [12]
Galewski, Alfred [13]
Rosenberg, Rubin [14]
Moszkowicz, Daniel [15]
Blones, Luszek
Elkiewicz, Elek
Mairowicz, Meir
Kanal, Israel
Fondaminski, Liba (Ala) [16]

[5] A leader of the Jewish partisan section in the Lublin region.
[6] A leader of the partisan section in the Lublin region.
[7] A member of the general staff of the United Organization of Partisans of the Vilna Ghetto; hanged by the Nazis.
[8] One of the leaders of the Treblinka revolt.
[9] Representative of the Jewish National Committee and the Jewish Fighting Organization in the Czestochowa Ghetto; killed during armed self-defense there.
[10] A liaison of the Jewish Fighting Organization working on the Aryan side.
[11] Benjamin Lejbgott, activist of the Polish Workers Party and Jewish Fighting Organization in the Warsaw Ghetto; felled during the armed self-defense of January.
[12] A fighter of the Chestochowa Ghetto.
[13] A leader of the Treblinka revolt.
[14] A fighter of the Bialystok Ghetto.
[15] Commander of armed self-defense in the Bialystok Ghetto.
[16] Wife of Ephraim Fondaminski, member of the Polish Workers Party and the Jewish Fighting Organization.

Lent, Szanin
Libeskind, Adolf [17]
Sznajdmil, Abram
Rozowski, Wolf
Ajger, Abram
Frydryck, Zygmunt
Frysztorf, Gabrys [18]
Szuster, Szlamek
Rotblat, Leyb (Lutek)
Fajkind, Mejlech
Folman, Marek [19]
Morgenstern, Jochanan [20]
Malinowski [21]

Michal Rola-Zymierski, Arms General
Commander-in-Chief of the Polish Army

Marian Spychalski, Brigadier General Deputy
Commander-in-Chief of the Polish Army for
Political Education Affairs

Trans. from Polish

[17] A member of the Jewish Fighting Organization command in the Warsaw Ghetto.
[18] A member of the Jewish Labor Bund and the Jewish Fighting Organization.
[19] Member of D'ror and officer of the People's Guard.
[20] Treasurer of the Jewish Fighting Organization of Warsaw, and Zionist activist.
[21] Member of the Jewish Labor Bund and of the Jewish Fighting Organization of Warsaw.

Postscript: The Historical and Moral Significance of the Warsaw Ghetto Uprising

The outcome of the modern-day confrontation between the Nazi "Goliath" and the Ghetto "David" bears little resemblance to its Biblical antecedent. This time, crude force and brutality prevailed. It was a gigantic struggle, though tragically unequal. For Hitler's Germany, it became an ignoble triumph: the image of a tiny band of fighters staving off for weeks and months the most powerful military machine ever known turned Nazi boasts into bitter disgrace. For Jews and all freedom-loving people, it was an unparalleled example of bravery in the face of imminent destruction. Thus the Warsaw Ghetto Uprising has great significance from two perspectives.

Historically, it was the first instance of urban resistance to the Nazi occupation. All other urban uprisings followed in its wake in 1944 and 1945, when the German armies had suffered crippling setbacks and the liberating Allied armies were already storming the gates of the occupied cities of eastern Europe. And the later revolts broke out in an atmosphere of popular agitation and ferment—carried on a wave of partisan struggle and sabotage; the Warsaw Ghetto Uprising occurred at a time when armed, organized revolt was still only a dream, and when partisan forces could be relied upon for only the most minimal aid. For Jews, the Uprising has even more significance. April 19, 1943, has become a great watershed—the dividing line between passivity, confusion, and despair in the face of annihilation and staunch determination to fight the invader to the last man.

Morally, the Ghetto revolt had both immediate and long-range repercussions. The example of a people fighting valiantly—though against overwhelming opposition—fired the spirits of the remnants of Jewish communities across Poland and far beyond its borders. We may justifiably say that all incidents of Jewish resistance and armed struggle that followed April 1943 were inspired in some way by the Warsaw Ghetto Uprising: the revolt in the Chestochowa Ghetto on June 25; armed resistance in the Bedzin Ghetto on August 1 and 2; the sabotage and riot in the Treblinka death camp on August 2; the uprising in the Bialystok Ghetto, which lasted from August 16 to about the end of the month; the revolt in the Sobibor death camp on August 14; and other acts of resistance carried on in the forests and countryside—as by the partisan brigade operating in the forest of Wyszkow that took the name of the Warsaw Ghetto hero Mordekhai Anielewicz.

News of the Warsaw Uprising reached the Vilna Ghetto, the Jewish fighters on the fronts, the Jewish rebels in France, and filled them with pride. Thus inspired, Hirsh Glick, a member of the United Partisan Organization in the Vilna Ghetto, composed his song "Never say you walk the final road," which became the hymn of the Jewish partisans and underground fighters.

There is no final road. Fight on with all your strength to the last breath. The Warwaw Ghetto fighters carried these words in their hearts even as they fell under the fire of Nazi bullets, as they were buried in the wrecked bunkers, as they suffocated from poison gas; as they stood alone and forsaken amid the fallen walls and raging fires. Even in their most tragic moments, they believed that this was not the final road for their people; their fortitude and courage was the noblest expression of the partisan slogan "In struggle you will find the road to life." Like the Biblical bush, the spirit they embodied burned with their bullet-riddled corpses—but was not consumed. It lights our road to the furthest reaches, an enduring symbol of moral strength for all times.

Sources [1]

Unpublished Documents

Archives of the Jewish Historical Institute
1. Ringelblum Archives, Sections I and II.
2. Collection of Documents of the Jewish National Committee and the Coordinating Commission of the Jewish Fighting Organization, the Bundist underground, and the brush factory area fighting groups.
3. Collection of reports of the Yiddisher Militerisher Farband.

Archives of the High Commission to Investigate Nazi War Crimes in Poland
1. Collection of citation proposals.
2. Files of legal proceedings against SS and Police Brig. Gen. Juergen Stroop and SS 2nd Lt. Franz Konrad.
3. Transcripts of the Stroop and Konrad trials.

Central Archives of the Interior Ministry
1. Archive of the Polish government-in-exile (Delegation) in London, File H458 (Jewish Affairs).
2. Archive of the Land Amy (A.K.), collection of reports of "Kalina" (Gen. Stefan Rowecki) to the Polish Delegation in London, June 1942 to April 1943.
3. Collection of materials of "Antek" (anti-Communist

---

[1] Documents listed here include only those dealing directly with the Warsaw Ghetto Uprising, omitting those concerned with the Warsaw Ghetto in general or with overall problems of the Jewish resistance movement.

agency); releases of "Rorwin," the espionage brigade, for 1943.

4. Collection of bulletins of the Polish police command *(Granatowa)* for 1943.

Archives of the Institute for Party History at the Central Committee of the Polish Workers Party

1. Collection of documents issued by People's Guard headquarters for 1943.
2. P.P.S. Central Committee collection of materials on espionage for 1943.
3. Collection of documents of the Internal Affairs Department at the Polish Delegation; reports on the political situation in Poland for 1943 and 1944.
4. Document folder of the Special Military Court, Case 46.

Archives of the State Museum at Majdenek
Marysia's *Warsaw Ghetto Dairy.*

Miscellaneous
Mordekhai Anielewicz's letters, from the Archives of the Jewish National Committee—now in the Archive of the Itzhak Ratzenelson Museum at Kibbutz Lokhaim Hagetaot in Israel—in possession of Dr. Adolf Berman, head of the J.N.C.

Published Documents

1. *The Report of Juergen Stroop*, published in French (Paris, 1946), in Polish (Warsaw, 1953; and in *Bulletin of the High Commission to Investigate Nazi War Crimes in Poland,* No. 11), in Yiddish (Warsaw, 1953), in English (Warsaw, 1958), in Hebrew (Jerusalem, 1959), and in German (Berlin, 1960).
2. M. Neistat, *Khurban v'mered gito varsha* (Tel-Aviv, 1947; also available in Yiddish) essentially contains battle reports of Itzhak Cukierman (Antek) and others, taken from the Ar-

chives of the Jewish National Committee, the second cables of the Jewish underground organizations in occupied Poland, biographies of fighters, and so on.

3. Philip Friedman, *Martyrs and Fighters* (New York, 1954), is a collection of published documents.

4. Ber Mark, *Documents and Materials on the Uprising in the Warsaw Ghetto* (Warsaw, 1953), includes documents mainly from the Ringelblum Archives, the Polish underground press, battle communications from the Central Archives of the Interior Ministry, and German archival material.

Underground Press

1. Maria Kann, *Na oczach swiata* (published secretly by Land Army circles in 1943), deals with battle events in the Ghetto.

2. Collection of the Polish Underground press in the third section of the Archives of the Institute for Party History of the Polish Workers Party.

Informal Accounts (verbal testimony, memoirs, statements)

1. Memoirs of Hersz Berlinski, the engineer Goldman, Ber Warm, and an anonymous writer "Shlomo"—all prepared in hiding on the Aryan side in 1944.

2. Memoirs written after the Polish liberation by Henryk Iwanski, Viktoria Iwanski, Gershon Alef (Bolek), Felix Oler, Joseph Brzezinski, Israel Gutman, Bernard Borg, Adolph Berman, Joseph Gibler-Barski, Jerzy Duracz, Wladyslaw Seidler, Michael Jaworski, Anthony Chruszczel (Monter), Richard Levi, Joseph Lehman, Joseph Malecki (Senk), Bronislaw Mirski, Victor Margolies, Kalman Mendelson, Jacob Putermilch, Masha Putermilch, Joshua Perchner, Joseph Celmeister, Simkha Korngold, David Klin, Cesary Ketling, Guta Rotenberg, Roman Sikorski, and Pola Szewski.[2]

[2] The author wishes to thank Cahim Lazia for his testimony and Captain Cesary Ketling for special documents.

Bibliography

Albert, J. *Yidishe varshe durkh payn, blut un toyt*. Buenos Aires, 1953.

Bartoszewski, W. "Acts of Solidarity at the Ghetto Walls" (Polish), in *Stolicza*, no. 5 (February 3, 1957).

Berland, M. *300 sha'ot b'geto*. Tel-Aviv, 1959.

Borzykowski, T. *Tsvishn falndike vent*. Warsaw, 1949.

Frimer, C. *Min hadlekah hahi*. Tel-Aviv, 1961.

Goldkorn, D. *Zikhrones fun an onteylnemerin in oyfshtand fun varshever geto*. Lodz, 1951.

Karmi, A. *Min hadlekah hahi*. Tel-Agiv, 1961.

Landau, L. *Chronicle of the War and Years of Occupation* (Polish). Warsaw, 1962.

Legec, S., and W. Legec. *Di zelner fun yidisher kampfs-organizatsye un zeyere fraynt*. Warsaw, 1953.

Lubetkin, T. *Akhronim al hakhomah*. Ein-Harod, 1946.

———. *Bime kilyon v'mered*. Ein-Harod, 1947.[1]

Mark, B. *Battle and Destruction of the War aw Ghetto* (Polish).[2] Warsaw, 1959.

Mark, B., and E. Mark. "P.P.R. and the Jewish Question During the Nazi Occupation" (Polish), in *Z Pola Walki*, no. 17 (1962).

Naiberg, A. *Haakhronim b'ketz hamered shel geto varshah*. Merhavia, 1958.

Peltel-Miedzyrzecka, F. *Fun beyde zaytn geto moyer*. New York, 1948.

Ron, D. *Hem yorim . . . Eliezer Geller, mifaked ezor b'geto varshah*. Tel-Aviv, 1960.

Trunk, I. *Gestaltn un gesheyenisn*. Buenos Aires, 1962.

---

[1] Translated into German as *Die Letzte Tage des Warschauer Getto*, with a foreword by Friedrich Wolf. East Berlin, 1949.

[2] Also translated into French, Spanish, Portuguese, Czech, and German.

Vdovinski, D. "Mered geto varshah," in *Hamashakif* (April 26, 1946).
Wolf, J. *Das dritte Reich und seine Vollstrecker* (German). West Berlin, 1961.

The following titles comprise a selected bibliography of some useful sources on the Warsaw Ghetto Uprising published in English. Those titles followed by an asterisk are available in paperback.

Apenszlak, Jacob, ed. *The Black Book of Polish Jewry*. New York: Roy Publishers, 1943.
Barkai, Meyer, ed. *Fighting Ghettos*.* New York: Tower, 1971.
Berg, Mary. *Warsaw Ghetto, A Diary*. New York: Fischer, 1945.
Donat, Alexander. *Holocaust Kingdom*. New York: Holt, Rinehart & Winston, 1965.
Edelman, Marek. *The Ghetto Fights*. New York: American Representation of the General Workers' Union of Poland, 1946.
Friedman, Philip, ed. *Martyrs and Fighters*. New York: Praeger, 1954.
Glatstein, Jacob, Israel Knox, and Samuel Margoshes, eds. *Anthology of Holocaust Literature*. Philadelphia: Jewish Publication Society, 1969.
Goldstein, Bernard. *The Stars Bear Witness*. New York: Viking, 1954.
Hersey, John. *The Wall* (novel). New York: Knopf, 1950.
Kaplan, Chaim. *Scroll of Agony*. New York: Macmillan, 1965.
Levin, Nora. *The Holocaust*.* New York: Schocken, 1973.
Meed, Vladka (Faygl Peltel-Miedzyrzecka). *On Both Sides of the Wall*. Tel-Aviv: Beit Lohamei Hagetaot and Hakibbutz Hameuchad Publishing House, 1973.
Ringelblum, Emmanuel. *Notes from the Warsaw Ghetto*,* edited by Jacob Sloan. New York: Schocken, 1974.
Suhl, Yuri, ed. *They Fought Back*.* New York: Schocken, 1975.
Trunk, Isaiah. *Judenrat*. New York: Macmillan, 1972.
Zylberberg, Michael. *A Warsaw Diary*. Bridgeport, Conn.: Hartmore, 1969.

Index